MW01141321

Staying on Fire in a Wet-Blanket World

RANDY PETERSEN

▼●◆■

RAY C. STEDMAN

David C. Cook Publishing Co. Elgin, Illinois—Weston, Ontario

Staying on Fire in a Wet-Blanket World

© 1992 David C. Cook Publishing Co.

Scripture quotations are from the Holy Bible, New International Version (NIV), © 1973, 1978, 1984 by International Bible Society. Used by permission of Zondervan Bible Publishers.

Published by David C. Cook Publishing Co.
850 North Grove Ave., Elgin, IL 60120
Cable address: DCCOOK
Designed by Randy Maid
Cover illustration by Guy Wolek
Inside illustrations by Bruce Van Patter
Printed in U.S.A.

ISBN: 0-7814-0004-X

C · O · N · T · E · N · T · S

ARE YOU READY FOR A CHRISTIAN LIFESTYLE?

Ever notice that you can swim along for years in the Christian life without leaving the shallow end of the pool? Then one day it hits you: If you're going to *do* anything about your faith, you've got to go deeper. If you're going to have a truly satisfying walk with God, you've got to plunge past surface spirituality, empty words, faith without action.

But you're wary. What will a really *Christian* lifestyle be like? Will you have to overcommit yourself? Will God demand the impossible of you? Will you have to erase your personality and become a musty, dusty saint from the pre-TV, pre-stereo, pre-microwave days?

Commitment for Today's Adults

Wary—that's how many of today's adults feel when they're urged to be "on fire for the Lord." They want to turn faith to action, but they've been raised to ask themselves, "What's in it for me?" They want to get serious about the Christian life—but in a new-fashioned way that works for them.

That's why we've introduced The Christian Lifestyle Series. It's designed to help today's adults "get real" about their commitment to Christ. Each course nudges them toward becoming more consistent disciples—without browbeating or boring them. Each session helps them to be honest about their struggles and take realistic, workable steps toward greater faithfulness.

Sessions for Today's Groups

Whether you lead a large Sunday School class or a small group, you know that today's adults hate five things:
- Boring lectures
- Lots of homework
- Being told what to think
- Subjects that have nothing to do with their everyday lives; and
- Courses that seem to go on forever.

The Christian Lifestyle Series lightens the load of lecture and increases active group participation. Each course offers reproducible student Resource sheets instead of requiring group members to read time-consuming, expensive student books. Each session asks for and respects group members' contributions and emphasizes real-life application. And instead of lasting twelve or thirteen weeks, each course wraps up in seven. If you want to fit a quarterly thirteen-week format, just combine two courses and skip the introductory session in one of them.

Format for Today's Leaders

Because you're busy, these sessions are easy to prepare and use. The step-by-step plans are easy to follow; instructions to the leader are in regular type, things you might say aloud are in bold type, and suggested answers are in parentheses.

A helpful article introduces the course, giving you an overview of the topic. The reproducible student Resource sheets are meant to be photocopied and handed out—or turn some into overhead projector transparencies if you like. Most sessions include a Resource sheet that will help prepare group members for your next meeting, too.

As always, feel free to adapt this course to the needs of your group. And may God use these sessions to help your group members discover the joy of a truly Christian lifestyle.

John Duckworth, Series Editor

SPIRITUAL SURVIVAL

By Ray C. Stedman

My home is on the Rogue River in southwestern Oregon. As the river flows by my door it is a quiet, happily murmuring stream. But ten miles downstream it turns into a raging torrent, sweeping through the walls of Hellgate Canyon with unbelievable power and white-capped display.

The varied assortment of rafters, kayakers, and boaters who challenge its course through the Coast Range have but one thought in mind—survival! A few hardy, experienced souls dare it on their own, but most rely on the river-wise guides who thoroughly know the dangers, can instruct in the techniques of survival, and are able to build implicit trust in their knowledge and leadership.

The Rapids of Life

By now you have doubtless discovered that life is very much like that powerful and treacherous river. Who hasn't felt at times that he or she is being carried along into unknown dangers quite beyond his or her control? Who hasn't breathed a sigh of relief during quiet seasons, only to have sudden intrusions of tragic circumstances press faith to the breaking point?

We've all known (and perhaps succumbed to) the allure of powerful temptations that can leave us shattered and disillusioned. Or we've thought we were doing okay, only to discover that we had badly misjudged our state and awakened too late to recover.

All these perils and more are charted for us in the seven letters to the churches of Asia, found in Revelation 2–3. The encouraging factor is that they come from the great River Guide Himself, Jesus our Lord. He thoroughly knows the dangers which confront us, and can advise knowledgeably and accurately of the correctives needed to survive. He also offers incredible rewards to those who make the trip successfully to the end.

Each of the seven letters confronts a different situation and teaches a different lesson.

Ephesus: Essentials

The first, to the church at Ephesus, describes the one absolutely essential motivation to survival. It is to preserve continuously the warm and intimate love for Jesus that we first felt when we learned of His agony of self-sacrifice on our behalf—the sacrifice which made salvation possible and brought us out of darkness into His marvelous light.

If we lose that love by being drawn into side currents of person-pleasing or self-gratification or personal ambition, we are in deadly danger of finding ourselves washed up on the shoals of life with little to show for having lived at all.

"Watch your motivation," says Jesus. "There is only one that can see you safely through the perils of life—a genuine and often-renewed love for Me."

Stand up, Smyrna!

The letter to Smyrna details quite a different danger. Here it is the terrible pressure to give up because faith will mean ridicule, ostracism, affliction, and outright persecution—even to the point of death.

We often think that difficulties and hard trials simply are to be part of our lot, but Jesus tells us that only these can build the moral strength and trust needed to get us through. Modern examples include Alexsandr Solzhenitsyn, who suffered for years in Soviet prisons and detention camps, but who was sustained by a deepening devotion to Christ. His sturdy declaration of truth has become a model to many of how one man can influence a whole generation.

We may believe that strong military forces are needed to preserve Christian civilization, but Smyrna teaches us that Jesus can keep His church alive and vigorous in the midst of social and political upheaval.

"Don't be intimidated by opposition!" cries Jesus. "Just as I died and came to life again, so can you, for the cross always leads to a crown!"

Peril in Pergamum

The letter to Pergamum stresses the need for integrity. The perils here are subtle. One of them is sexual seduction.

A young businessman once told me of being with associates in a city away from home. His two friends planned to go out and find women for a sexual party, but being a Christian he demurred and stayed in the room to write letters. After going to bed, he was awakened by his two friends who were returning with *three* women. One of the women promptly climbed in bed with him, awakening strong physical response. But he reminded himself of all he had to lose, and what his Lord would think—and wisely dressed without a word of reproach and went down to get another room.

The other peril at Pergamum was to seek personal power at the price of integrity. This was the doctrine of the Nicolaitans. It is found in many offices today in the lure of the "inner circle," entrance to which demands some surrender of moral principle.

"But," says Jesus, "don't forget that integrity maintained means greater intimacy with Me. Guard your morality with care!"

The Threat to Thyatira

The letter to Thyatira develops the other side of the same problem. It teaches us that compromise destroys.

Under the figure of the Old Testament queen, Jezebel, who introduced idolatry into Israel, a newer Jezebel teaches Christians that having another god is necessary to do business in the modern world. The letter warns against adopting the world's value system in place of the personal honesty which Christ requires. To lie, to shade principle, to promise what can't be delivered, is to begin a downward slide into moral disaster.

The late 1980s' spate of indictments for insider trading on Wall Street was a case in point. Those indicted testified to the way their moral perceptions were blunted by the lust for easy money. The result: prison. In the same way, a false god leads to certain destruction.

"But remember," Jesus urges, "faithfulness leads to greater authority. He who overcomes will reign with Me."

Sardis: Sinking

Sardis is the church in deepest trouble. It started well, but soon began to lean on a good reputation. That led to coasting. Before the Christians at Sardis knew it they were all but dead.

The Lord's staccato command to them is, "Wake up! Strengthen what remains." The lesson to each of us is clear: words are never enough. A reputation for past success will soon disappear if the deeds that built it are missing.

This letter is a call for consistency: Begin again where you once were. Apathy and lethargy are deadly enemies, so recognize them as such and come alive.

"Those who do," says Jesus, "will find security and honor. Limited success is far better than phony achievement."

Faithful Philadelphia

Alone among the churches, the church of Philadelphia merits the full approval of its Lord, without reproach of any kind. It is because its members are alert to their opportunities, compassionate to their enemies, and patiently aware that nothing will ever be fully set right until Jesus comes.

Read the lives of the heroes and heroines of the church and see how that pattern is repeated in each life. With the love of Jesus as a continuing motive, and a determination to faithfully reflect His character until He returns, men and women like Jim Elliott, Amy Carmichael, and thousands unnamed have earned the title, "of whom the world was not worthy."

"I will acknowledge them as My own," Jesus declares, "in new ways they cannot now imagine!"

Lukewarm Laodicea

Laodicea is the church filled with self-sufficient members. They had two problems.

First, there was a lack of full commitment; they were neither hot nor cold. Second, there was an inaccurate self-image; they thought they were rich when they were really poor. They were comfortable and complacent. But in the eyes of Jesus they were far from what He wanted His people to be.

The church is not a country club, operated for the benefit of its members. It is not a performing arts center, offering high-quality entertainment. It is not a political action group, choosing up sides in the public arena. It is not a protest movement, radically seeking the overthrow of law and order. What it is intended to be is salt, and salty salt at that, flavoring life and arresting its corruption. And it is to be light, widely visible light, illuminating a dark and confused world.

To help the church be this, Jesus offers Himself in intimate and personal relationship to be the source of all that's needed for ministry. "Nothing else will suffice," He says. "Only My life lived through your life will do the trick. It will bring you through the shoals and rapids of life to share with Me in the final triumph!"

Can you make it through the dangers, toils, and snares of this dangerous world? Of course you can—if you love your Leader, heed His warnings, and lay hold of His resources. Without Him you cannot succeed; with Him you cannot fail!

REMEMBER YOUR FIRST LOVE?
Learning from the Church at Ephesus

The Ephesians had a star church. Paul had a special fondness for these people, staying with them two years and writing them a tender epistle. He even made a point of meeting with the Ephesian elders during a layover on one journey home.

Timothy was appointed as pastor of this church, and Paul wrote him two more epistles. Tradition has it that the apostle John landed at Ephesus as a senior elder in the waning days of his life. It's as if Billy Graham, Luis Palau, and John Stott all ministered at the same church! What status that church would have!

But something happened along the way. The superchurch got so involved in fighting heresy, holding fast to the truth, maintaining a solid church organization, and so on, that it forgot the basics—the love of Jesus Christ.

That can easily happen to us, too. In the rush to fight New Age teachings and permissiveness, are Christians also rushing to love Jesus more? As we apply church growth principles to market our programs, are we reaching out in His love to others?

Love is a basic. That's where staying "on fire" starts. And that's what your group can learn from the example of the Ephesians.

Where You're Headed:
To remind your group members of the centrality of love for Christ and showing His love to others.

Scriptures You'll Apply:
Revelation 1:9-11, 17, 18; 2:1-7

Things You'll Need:
- Bibles
- Pens or pencils
- Copies of "Destination: Ephesus" (Resource 1)
- Copies of "Love and Action" (Resource 2)
- Two copies of "The Other Side" (Resource 3)
- Two people prepared to read the drama on Resource 3
- Index cards
- Copies of Resource 4, "Destination: Smyrna" (optional)

1
Remember When?

Thinking about Being in Love

Ask a man and a woman to stand in front of the group. They'll be playing the role of a fictional couple, Chad and Natalie.

This is Chad and Natalie. They just got married five minutes ago. Needless to say, they're very close.

Time passes. Now Chad and Natalie have been married for three years. What are some things that might have come between them during that time? (Routine, arguments over money, birth of children, etc.)

With each item named, have the man and woman move further apart. Ask the same question about the couple at ten years and twenty years into their marriage, moving them further and further apart.

Then ask: **Chad, do you feel as close to Natalie as you did when you were first married? How about you, Natalie?**

Chances are that something will have changed about their sense of closeness. If not, press them for their secret of staying close despite distractions. Then thank them for their help and move on to group discussion.

If you've ever been in love, think back to the beginning of that relationship. What was love like at first? How did it grow?

After some have answered, try this question: **Have you ever "forgotten" about love? Did you reach a point where you were just going through the motions of a relationship and you didn't know why?**

Since this is a very personal question, you don't need to hear answers—but let people think about it.

If needed, observe that even though real love is not just a feeling, actions that were begun in love can lose their moorings. Feelings of love are not all-important, but they can help keep us properly directed.

Next question: **Have you ever been in love with God?**
What is it like? How does it compare with human love?
Read Revelation 2:2-4 to the group.
What does it mean to "forsake your first love"?
How can we avoid that?
We'll talk about all that, but first we need some background.

2
Superchurch

Learning the Background
of the Ephesian Church

Hand out Resource 1, "Destination: Ephesus."

Ask: **What do you think of when I say, "The Book of Revelation"?** (Most will think of prophecy about the end times.)

Ask someone to read Revelation 1:9-11.

Who's the author? (John.)

Who's John? (An apostle. One of Jesus' closest three disciples, "the disciple whom Jesus loved.") Ask the group to begin filling out Resource 1.

From where was he writing, and why? (From the island of Patmos. He was exiled there because of his church leadership, probably during the reign of Roman Emperor Domitian [A.D. 81-95]. It was common for the Romans to treat leaders of subversive groups in this way.)

To whom was the Book of Revelation written? (The seven churches listed in Revelation 2.)

Where were these churches? (In the area that is now Turkey. This area had been evangelized by Paul and probably others—40 to 50 years earlier.)

Ask someone to read Revelation 1:17, 18.

If we had to boil down the theme of Revelation to one phrase, it would be this: "God is in control." This is something these seven churches needed to know. They were in different situations—some rich, some poor, some persecuted, some doing okay. But all of them needed to know that God was in charge of their world.

Have someone read Revelation 2:1.

Verses 8, 12, 18, and 3:1, 7, 14 start the same way. Each of the seven churches gets a special message from the Lord. Over the next seven weeks we'll look at these messages to see what we can learn about staying on fire in a wet-blanket world.

What do you know about this first church, Ephesus?

As needed, add the following points to the discussion:

• Paul started the church, and wrote an epistle to it.

• Timothy served there.

• John lived there late in his life.

• Ephesus was the fourth largest city in the Roman Empire at the time, a center of trade and wealth and of the worship of Artemis, a local fertility goddess.

• In the Book of Ephesians, Paul mentioned that the church there had faith and love; he prayed that they would have wisdom, the knowledge of God, and the fullness of God's love. He saw them growing in truth and love; they would avoid false teaching and love each other.

Ask someone to read Revelation 2:2-5.

John is writing this probably thirty years after Paul wrote his epistle. How were the Ephesians doing? What were they excelling in? (Hard work, withstanding persecution, holding to the truth.)

Now ask someone to read verses 4 and 5.

What was wrong? What was missing? (Their "first love." This could mean either love for God or love for people, and probably both. Remember the picture in Ephesians of a loving congregation.)

How serious a problem was this? (Quite serious; it required repentance.)

What did the Ephesians need to do? (Remember their previous state and repent—get back to it!)

3
The Love Connection

(15 minutes)

Showing How We Can
Forget the Reasons Behind
the Good Things We Do

Hand out: Resource 2, "Love and Action."

Answer these first three questions as honestly as you can. You won't be handing in these papers, so no one else will see your answers.

Give people a few minutes to answer the first three questions. Then read through "The Four Stages."

Have you seen this sort of thing happen in others? Why do you think this happens?

Divide the group four ways. Assign each team one of the following.

Team A: Reading the Bible and praying every morning

Team B: Singing in the choir

Team C: Driving the youth group van to retreats and other events

Team D: Handing out food at a local food pantry each week

Each of these is a perfectly good activity. But if it goes through "The Four Stages," it can go astray. As a team, take a couple of minutes to figure out what might happen if a person kept doing this activity while losing the original motivation. Then send one or more representatives up to the front to act out (in pantomime) what you came up with. Have someone read your four stages as they're acted out.

An example to get people started:

Stage 1: A man starts teaching Sunday school out of love for the Lord. He works hard to prepare, prays, and keeps the class interested with his sincerity, knowledge, and example.

Stage 2: The man teaches to be religious. He keeps preparing, but stops praying because he is less concerned about real spiritual results.

Stage 3: The man teaches out of habit. He shows up, but doesn't prepare much. The class is getting bored.

Stage 4: He teaches for what he can get out of it. When the bored class doesn't participate, he gets disgusted and quits.

After the pantomimes are acted out, ask the questions from the bottom of Resource 2: **At which stage do you find yourself? How have your actions changed?**

Let people just think about these if they don't wish to answer aloud.

4
A Second Opinion
(5 minutes)

Understanding the Ephesian Situation and Comparing It to Ours

Let's take another look at the Ephesian church and see how things might have gotten to this point.

Have two "actors" present the material on Resource 3, "The Other Side."

Afterward, make sure the group realizes that this is conjecture, an idea of how things *might* have been.

Is this a realistic scenario?

How might this sort of thing happen in a modern church? (Much the same way, really. An over-attention to doctrinal or behavioral purity, to the point that love is forgotten. Love must remain the reason behind the purity.)

5
Strategy for Survival
(10 minutes)

Planning Specific Ways to Keep Our "First Love"

How do you hang onto your first love?
Read Revelation 2:5.
What three things were the Ephesians told to do? (Remember; repent; do.)

This can serve as an outline for our strategy of keeping our first love. But how can you flesh these three things out?
Form small groups. Give each group an index card.

Let's say a person has come to you and said, "This is me; I've left my first love. I'm just going through the motions now. I don't seem to love God or others as I should. What should I do?"

Talk together in your groups to find a three-part course of action for such a person. Write "Remember," "Repent," and "Do" on the card I've given you. Now figure out *how*. What should a person remember and when and how often?

How can a person indicate that he or she is truly sorry for the decline?

And what "first things" should a person do to get back on track?

Give groups five minutes to meet together. Then have each group report to the whole group.

Wrap things up like this: **If you've left your first love, maybe there's some advice on your card that you can take for yourself. I urge you to take that next step toward drawing close to the Lord again. If you do, He'll draw near to you.**

Close in prayer, thanking God for the love He has put in your hearts, and confessing ways in which you have forsaken that love. Offer to talk later with any who want to rekindle their "fire" for the Lord.

If you'd like to prepare people for next time, hand out copies of Resource 4, "Destination: Smyrna." Encourage group members to work through it, using any Bible study helps they may have as well as Scripture itself.

DESTINATION: EPHESUS

RESOURCE 1

The Book of Revelation

Author:

Written from:

Circumstances:

Recipients:

Theme:

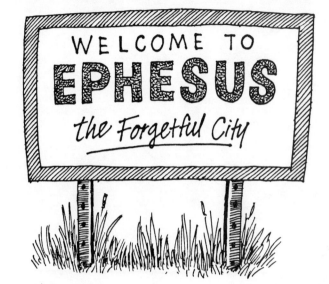

WELCOME TO
EPHESUS
the Forgetful City

The Ephesus File

Background: Biblical people involved there: _____, _____, _____.

Fourth largest city in Roman Empire, known for trade, wealth, worship of Artemis (Diana)

Hallmarks of the Ephesian church in Paul's time: _____

_____

_____

_____

_____

From the text:

How does Christ describe Himself?

What does He "know"?

Course of action:

LOVE AND ACTION

1. What actions have you done in the last week to show your love for God?

2. What actions have you done in the last week to show your God-given love for others?

3. Think back to the first six months that you were a Christian. How did your love-actions then differ from your love-actions now?

_____ More emotional then
_____ More mature now
_____ More active then
_____ I know what I'm doing now
_____ I'm more selfish now
_____ I'm bored now
_____ Keeps getting better all the time
_____ Other _____

The Four Stages

Stage 1: We do acts of devotion and charity out of love for God.

Stage 2: The love fades. We still do these acts out of a desire to be religious.

Stage 3: We continue to do these acts out of habit. Sometimes we are less faithful about doing them.

Stage 4: We do these acts to please ourselves, to give us status, strokes, etc. We change what we do in order to meet our own needs.

At which stage do you find yourself? How have your actions changed?

THE OTHER SIDE

(Two members of the Ephesian church speak to audience.)

AQUILA: The Book of Revelation says some critical things about our church, and we can accept that . . .

PRISCILLA: But we think you ought to hear our side of the story. There are an awful lot of good things about our church. Even John would agree with that.

AQUILA: And this thing about "forsaking our first love"—well, it's very understandable when you know the whole story.

PRISCILLA: The church started out really great. When Paul was here, and right after he left, the church was known for its love.

AQUILA: If you needed anything, someone here could meet that need. We were really caring for each other.

PRISCILLA: And we had the greatest worship services. We would sing and listen to the Scriptures and pray together.

AQUILA: It was exciting to meet with the church. We were all . . . so crazy about the Lord.

PRISCILLA: But then we started to have problems. These guest speakers started showing up, claiming that they were sent by Paul or by the apostles in Jerusalem. So we listened to them, at first.

AQUILA: But after a while it became clear that they were twisting the Scriptures. They weren't preaching the truth about Jesus.

PRISCILLA: So we had to ask them to leave. It was tough. Some people in the church didn't agree and they left, too. It put a damper on things. And then there was the problem with the Artemis worshipers.

AQUILA: Oh, yes. We got a number of people coming over to us who used to worship Artemis, the local fertility goddess.

PRISCILLA: It seemed they wanted to keep some of their old immoral ways.

AQUILA: They claimed to follow Christ, but their behavior was the same as before. They were influencing some of our young people.

PRISCILLA: We finally had to spell it out to them. The old ways have to go. When you become a Christian, you're a new person.

AQUILA: So all of that caused some problems, too. All of a sudden we were looking at everyone's behavior, checking up on everyone.

PRISCILLA: I remember once I was talking with an old friend of mine in the marketplace. She'd gotten involved with Artemis worship, and I was trying to draw her into the church. But then I saw someone else from our church coming toward us—and I stopped the conversation and moved away. I didn't want to be seen with this pagan person because I was afraid of what other Christians would think. Isn't that awful? I'm ashamed of that now . . .

AQUILA: But that's the kind of spirit we began to have in the church. We were holding the line on doctrine, on behavior.

PRISCILLA: We were determined to be a righteous and pure church.

AQUILA: We stopped singing some of our favorite hymns, because they were borrowed from the Greek religions. We examined everything that was said or done in a service, so that it was theologically proper.

PRISCILLA: Which is good, isn't it? I mean, we do have to be true to God's truth, don't we?

AQUILA: And that's all we really wanted to say. To be honest, we do feel something's missing.

PRISCILLA: That love we had, for each other and for God—I miss it. But sometimes you've got to do what you've got to do.

DESTINATION: SMYRNA

WELCOME TO SMYRNA
the Suffering City

From a Commentary or Study Bible
Background on Smyrna:

From the text (Revelation 2:8-11)
How does Christ describe Himself?

What does He "know"?

Course of action:

COME HELL OR HIGH WATER
Learning from the Church at Smyrna

Sometimes it's hard to identify with first-century Christians. They were persecuted in cruel ways for their faith. Most of us are not. Much of the scriptural encouragement for the persecuted remains hypothetical for us. *If we were* persecuted, would we be faithful?

We can deal with this in three ways:

1. *Assume that we must not be living right.* If we were truly righteous, this line of reasoning goes, we'd be persecuted. Push this to the extreme and you may get a bunch of obnoxious Christians, buttonholing and haranguing and pestering others. "Come on! I dare you! Persecute me!" They may get the persecution they seek, but it's not for their faith. They're just obnoxious. Meeker believers, meanwhile, fall victim to unnecessary guilt.

2. *Decide that we* are *being persecuted.* "Look at the snide comments on TV!" we say. "Look at the legal decisions on school prayer!" Are Western Christians a persecuted minority? *Maybe* things are headed that way, but we still enjoy great religious freedom. We seldom recognize the power we have. To say we're "persecuted" because we can't put a nativity scene in the city park may be watering down the idea of persecution.

3. *Thank God for the freedom we have, but be careful.* Watch out for the undercurrents in our society—the worship of sex, money, or power. The adherents of these "false religions" may never arrest and imprison us for our faith, but they may isolate us, slander us, or prevent our professional advancement. These subtler forms of "persecution" should not surprise us or dishearten us. The teachings of Revelation 2:8-11, and the example of Smyrna, can help us cope.

Where You're Headed:
To alert your students to the possibility of being persecuted in various ways for their faith, and to encourage them to remain faithful to Christ.

Scriptures You'll Apply:
Revelation 2:8-11

Things You'll Need:
- Bibles
- Pens or pencils
- Copies of "Good News, Bad News" (Resource 5) for two actors only
- Copies of "A Short History of Persecution" (Resource 6)
- Copies of "Because I'm a Christian . . ." (Resource 7)
- Prepare two group members to do drama on Resource 5
- Copies of Resource 8, "Destination: Pergamum" (optional)

1
Good News/ Bad News

(10 minutes)

Reviewing Our Response
to Persecution

Start by having two group members present the skit from Resource 5, "Good News, Bad News."

Then ask: **Did you identify with this guy at all? Do you ever feel guilty for not being persecuted?**

Why do you think we are not generally persecuted for our faith in this society? (Some may say that Christians aren't serious enough, but be sure this point is raised: In His grace, God has allowed us a greater degree of religious freedom than many societies have known. We can be thankful for this gift from God.)

Have you ever been persecuted for your faith? In what way? If there are few responses, broaden it slightly: **Have you ever been put at a disadvantage because of your faith? Have others ever hated or shunned you merely because you were a Christian?**

2
The First and Last Word

(15 minutes)

Analyzing Christ's
Message to Smyrna

Whether or not you're persecuted, the *fear* **of persecution can have a wet-blanket effect on your spiritual fire. That was the Lord's message to the church at Smyrna.**

Invite group members to dig out Resource 4, "Destination: Smyrna," if you handed it out last time.

We don't know a lot about Smyrna. But we know a few things.

1. The city was a major one, about forty miles north of Ephesus but not quite as big. It was a bustling seaport and a center of wealth and science.

2. Smyrna was very cozy with Rome. Many Roman citizens lived there. Whereas Ephesus was the center of worship for the local goddess, Smyrna was a center of emperor-worship. In John's time, Emperor Domitian had declared himself a god and required all citizens to perform a sacrifice to him, saying, "Caesar is Lord." (This was mostly a political commitment in religious trappings, but most Christians saw it as idolatry.) Once you performed the sacrifice, you would get a certificate. Without that certificate, you were subject to discrimination and possibly punishment.

3. There was also a substantial Jewish community in Smyrna. Although Jews and Christians coexisted peaceably in some areas, this was not the case in Smyrna. Well into the second century, the Jews were strong opponents of the Smyrna church.

Ask someone to read Revelation 2:8, 9. Ask: **How does Jesus, who's dictating this letter, describe Himself?** (The First and the Last, who died and came to life again.)

Why might this be important to the Christians there? (Christ was around before the Emperor and would be around long afterward. He had conquered death. Here was the promise of resurrection for the threatened believers.)

What does Jesus say He "knows" about the Smyrna situation? (Their affliction, their poverty, and the slander against them.)

What does He mean by, "Yet you are rich!"? (Spiritually rich in Christ, though materially poor.)

If Smyrna was such a wealthy city, why were the Christians poor? (Very likely, there was economic persecution. Christians would lose their jobs, their businesses, their lands. This was often the first step of Roman persecution.)

Who were "those who say they are Jews and are not"? (There are a few possibilities:

[1] He could be saying that Christians are now the "true Jews." If the purpose of Judiasm was to lead people to Christ, then those who reject Christ would in a sense no longer be "real" Jews. Paul said something similar in Romans 2:28, 29.

[2] He could be saying that there was a pocket of troublemakers causing problems for the church. They were not true Jews because they violated their own law in "bearing false witness" against the church. They no longer sought to serve God, but were serving Satan.

[3] Perhaps there were Christians who claimed to be Jews in order to avoid sacrificing to the emperor, since Jews sometimes were exempted from such requirements. But it's difficult to see how these would "slander" the church, unless they were claiming that the Lordship of Christ didn't matter.)

What could this "slander" involve? (There were many false ideas of Christians, some circulated by persecutors. They were accused of cannibalism [eating flesh and drinking blood at Communion], incest [love between "brothers and sisters"], and treason [meeting in secret to promote the kingdom of God].)

In what ways are Christians slandered today? (Some say Christians are emotionally disturbed, uncaring, power-hungry, hypocritical, only after money, etc.)

Ask someone to read verse 10. Ask: **How should Christians react to persecution?** (Don't be afraid, be faithful.)

What is the "ten days" thing all about? (It could be a literal prediction of some ten-day reign of terror. Or it may have symbolic meaning; if each hour is a year, then ten days could correspond to the 240 years or so before Emperor Constantine would stop persecution. Most likely, however, it simply stands for "a short time.")

What does Christ promise to those who are faithful to the point of death? (A crown of life.)

Why would this appeal to those in Smyrna? (A crown of laurel was given to those who won races. They would have won the race of life. Also, their persecutor, Emperor Domitian, wore a crown; in the next life, the Christians would reign.)

Ask someone to read verse 11. Ask: **How does someone "overcome"?** (By remaining faithful to Christ despite persecution.)

What is the "second death"? (Spiritual death, hell, separation from God for eternity.)

Why would this encourage the Christians at Smyrna? (They would be facing deadly persecution, and this puts it in perspective. The first death is not the end; there is another life to come.)

3
Enemies: A Love Story

(10 minutes)

Recapping the History
of Church Persecution

Hand out copies of Resource 6, "A Short History of Persecution." Have several readers read it aloud, a few paragraphs at a time.

Ask: **Did you learn anything from this?**

What was new to you?

How should we respond when we hear of Christians in other lands being persecuted for their faith? (Pray, help in any way possible, push political leaders to change things, learn from them.)

4
Are We Persecuted?

(15 minutes)

Considering the
Opposition We Face,
and How to Deal With It

Hand out Resource 7, "Because I'm a Christian . . ."

Divide into three groups. Have each group read over the situations listed and talk about what to say to the characters. (If you're running late, assign one or two situations to each group.)

After five minutes or so, bring groups back together and review the five situations.

Were these people really being persecuted for their faith?

What advice did you give them?

(Situations C and E are iffy. It is possible that they brought the situations on themselves by expressing their Christianity in inappropriate ways at inappropriate times. One might advise them to look for more appropriate opportunities for sharing their faith. But still, it is not surprising that any of these people encounter opposition for being true to their faith.)

How might the *fear* of persecution influence the way these characters act in the future?

How has the fear of criticism affected the way you talk about God with non-Christians? The way you live out your faith in other ways?

If you had no fear of being teased or looked down on for your faith, how might your life be different?

You might conclude with comments like these: **Persecutors in our society might not arrest you or execute you—but they may mock you, lie about you, or make you lose your job. Our society supposedly tolerates any belief, but true Christianity is still pretty shocking when it's consistently applied.**

God has a whole new life waiting for us. When it comes to staying on fire spiritually, it's His opinion that counts most.

Close in prayer, asking God for strength when our faith puts us at a disadvantage in today's world. Also, pray for those believers around the world who are suffering for their faith.

If you'd like to prepare people for next time, hand out copies of Resource 8, "Destination: Pergamum." Encourage group members to work through it, using any Bible study helps they may have as well as Scripture itself.

GOOD NEWS, BAD NEWS

B: Hey, friend, why are you looking so glum?

> **A:** I'm a Christian and I'm not being persecuted.

B: Well, that's good news!

> **A:** No, it's bad.

B: Why?

> **A:** Because Christians are supposed to be persecuted. The world hates those who follow Christ and it torments them.

B: Oh, that's bad.

> **A:** No, it's good.

B: Why?

> **A:** Because Christians grow through persecution. They trust more fully in Christ and He comforts those who turn to Him in trouble.

B: That's good.

> **A:** No, it's bad—because I'm not being persecuted. I must not be living a good Christian life.

B: That's . . . uh . . . good?

> **A:** No, it's bad! It's terrible! I feel so guilty.

B: *That's* bad.

> **A:** No, actually, that's *good*, because guilt motivates me. I will strive to live better because I feel such inadequacy.

B: Is that good or bad?

> **A:** If you don't know by now, I'm certainly not going to tell you. Listen, I've got to run. Good night.

B: What's so good about it?

A SHORT HISTORY OF PERSECUTION

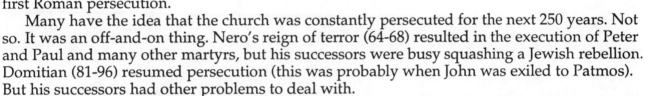

The earliest persecution of Christians came from their fellow Jews. The Book of Acts records much of this—Stephen's stoning, James's execution, Peter's imprisonment. At that point, the Romans didn't care much about Christianity; they considered it all a Jewish squabble. In fact, the apostle Paul used Roman influence to save him from Jewish persecution.

The Jews had long enjoyed a certain tolerance from Rome, and Christianity had thrived under that blanket of protection. But now, more and more Gentiles were joining the church. By the 60s A.D., the Romans were beginning to figure out that Christianity wasn't the same as Judaism—and that made it an "illicit religion." When much of Rome was burned in a fire, Emperor Nero blamed the Christians and launched the first Roman persecution.

Many have the idea that the church was constantly persecuted for the next 250 years. Not so. It was an off-and-on thing. Nero's reign of terror (64-68) resulted in the execution of Peter and Paul and many other martyrs, but his successors were busy squashing a Jewish rebellion. Domitian (81-96) resumed persecution (this was probably when John was exiled to Patmos). But his successors had other problems to deal with.

Christianity continued to be officially illegal, but some officials turned a blind eye. Rashes of persecution would flare up in local areas for a few years at a time—Asia Minor, Gaul, North Africa. This created a sort of ebb and flow that was actually healthy for the church. Persecution would strengthen the church by weeding out the pretenders and inspiring the faithful. Some great leaders were lost, but others stepped in to fill the gap. It was a pruning process.

There was actually a time in the early 200s when the emperor was friendly toward Christianity. Church buildings were constructed. The church met openly. In fact, it grew so much that, around 250, Emperor Decius decided that Christians were a threat to the empire. He launched a systematic persecution, first taking property away, then arresting church leaders, then killing them. Fifty years later, after another period of calm, Diocletian launched the last great Roman persecution of the church. It lasted ten years, with an unprecedented viciousness. But the church withstood it. By 311, Christianity was declared a legal religion. By 325, under Constantine, it was the official religion of the empire.

Of course, new problems arose. Christians began to bicker with each other. There were sometimes violent confrontations between rival groups. Christians fought to the death for their view of Christianity, for the right to meet with their group, for the right to translate the Bible into the language of the people, for political power.

In modern times, Christians have undergone serious persecution under Communist regimes. In Eastern Europe and the Soviet Union, the church has outlasted those regimes. As of this writing, the church in China remains constrained, though the dismal days of the Cultural Revolution (1966-76) are past. Reports from China indicate the existence of a remarkably strong underground church that withstood the scourges of the Maoists during that violent decade. But, given the history of Christianity under persecution, that is hardly surprising. God gives strength in tough times.

Situation A: FRANCIS

Every day I face pressure to do things that are unethical. I'm in business, managing a division of a major company. I have been encouraged to lie, to betray people, to falsify tax reports, to break promises—all in order to be "loyal" to the company. I have tried to be faithful to the Lord through all this. In fact, I've told my boss, "I can't do that, I'm a Christian." I truly believe this has kept me out of the "inner circle" at this company. I'd be a vice-president now if I went along with the flow. Sometimes I resent that, but maybe I'm lucky to have a job at all.

What would you say to Francis?

Situation B: BECKY

I think I'm the only person at my college who's still a virgin. I'm a senior now, and it hasn't been easy, but I made up my mind to honor the Lord with my sexuality. I'm waiting till marriage. It's not something I talk about a lot, but I let my "secret" out to a friend and now all the girls in my dorm think I'm strange. And most of the guys stay away from me, unless they're trying to make some big "conquest." I really hate the way they tease me, but I guess it's worth it.

What would you say to Becky?

Situation C: EVELYN

I've taught fifth grade for 35 years, and I'm alarmed at the changes I've seen. Children today are growing up without any direction, without morality. When I started teaching, we had a time of prayer and Bible reading each day. I thought that was nice. But now we can't do that anymore. Still I've tried to inject a little Bible into the class work. I often start my class by reading sections from the Psalms. Apparently some atheist parent complained about this. Now the principal tells me I have to stop it. I'm not sure what to do.

What would you say to Evelyn?

Situation D: KATHERINE

I work as a waitress at a pretty nice restaurant. The salary is low, but the tips are great. The other waitresses tell me they only report about a third of their tip money on their taxes. It's all cash; they'll never get caught. I said I couldn't do that because I'm a Christian. But now they're all mad at me, because if I report all my tips the IRS will know they're underreporting. I don't want to hurt them, but I have to be honest, right? Some of the other waitresses aren't speaking to me.

What would you say to Katherine?

Situation E: TODD

Sharing the Gospel seems to come easily to me. I'll meet people and 30 seconds later I'm telling them about God's love. I've been working at this bookstore, where the other employees were turned off by my Christianity. I knew they made fun of me behind my back. But customers didn't seem to mind when I talked about God. Last week, however, my boss fired me. She said my work was okay; she just didn't want me preaching to the customers. It was bad for the store's image, she said. I guess I should expect that kind of persecution.

What would you say to Todd?

DESTINATION: PERGAMUM

WELCOME TO **PERGAMUM** *the Gullible City*

From a Commentary or Study Bible
Background on Pergamum:

From the text (Revelation 2:12-17)
How does Christ describe Himself?

What does He "know"?

Course of action:

DON'T BE DECEIVED
Learning from the Church at Pergamum

It's amazing how similar the New Testament world is to ours.

When John wrote down Jesus' message to the seven churches, the Roman world was in the midst of a sort of New Age Movement. Cults from the East, from Egypt, from the hills beyond Pergamum, were sweeping through the Mediterranean world. People were spiritually hungry, but not spiritually disciplined. Many of these cults involved sexual rites. Some promoted excessive use of wine or drugs. The traditional gods of Rome were given lip service, but little else.

Does any of this sound familiar? Nowadays *our* God is the traditional one. People pay lip service, but observe other priorities in their daily lives. They are spiritually hungry, but they ignore the true Source of life. Instead they dabble in astrology, spiritualism, eastern philosophies—or worship the secular trinity of money, sex, and power.

Pergamum had people *within the church* who were succumbing to false teaching. The same thing is happening to Christians today. This should be a session to shake some people awake, to point our compass toward the truth.

Where You're Headed:
To warn your students of the danger of false teaching and to reorient them toward God's truth.

Scriptures You'll Apply:
Revelation 2:12-17

Things You'll Need:
• Bibles
• Pens or pencils
• Copies of "What Do You Think?" (Resource 9)
• Copy of "The Power of the Air" (Resource 10) for someone who is prepared to act it out (Consider putting this on video to play for the group)
• Copies of "Scripture List" (Resource 11)
• Copies of Resource 12, "Destination: Thyatira" (optional)

1
True or False

(10 minutes)

Examining What
Our World Believes

Hand out Resource 9, "What Do You Think?"

Note that this is no ordinary true-false test. In addition to the space for your own opinion, there is a space to write "what most of the people you know would say." Give the group a few minutes to fill out both columns. Then talk through it, paying attention to both columns. Ask people what they put and why.

1. It doesn't matter what you believe, as long as you're nice to people. (A lot of people think this, but it's false. Being nice to people is important, but belief in Christ is all-important.)

2. If you do good in this life, you will be reincarnated as a good person in the next. (Reincarnation has many adherents, and many other dabblers, but the Bible does not support it. The Bible certainly has no "merit system" like this. People live, die, and go to heaven or hell.)

3. Belief in Jesus is the only way to get to heaven. (True. A lot of people think this is very narrow-minded, but this is what the New Testament says.)

4. After you die, there's nothing else. (False. The Bible speaks of an afterlife, with or without God.)

5. Sexual relations should be reserved for marriage. (True. Not a popular view these days, but the Bible clearly presents this as what God wants.)

6. Astrology can help guide your life. (Many believe this, and many others dabble in it, but the Bible warns against guiding your life by the stars.)

7. The Bible is God's Word. (That's what the Bible claims to be. The idea is foreign to many unbelievers.)

8. If you're good in this life, you'll go to heaven. (Nope. This may be common sense, but it's not biblical. We're saved by God's grace, not by the good things we do.)

9. God wants us to share our wealth with those in need. (Yes. Some unbelievers might even agree with this. And yet many Christians find it hard to do.)

10. The most important thing in life is to have a good time. (No. Pleasing God is most important—and having a good time doing it. Many today follow a hedonistic philosophy, both within and outside the church.)

Then discuss:

Which of the mistaken ideas on this sheet do you think are influencing Christians today?

How do you sort the true from the false?

2
Sharpening That Sword
(15 minutes)

Analyzing Christ's Message
to Pergamum

We aren't the only ones who have to deal with warped ideas. The church in Pergamum was the same way.

If you passed out copies of Resource 8, "Destination: Pergamum," last time, ask any who filled them out to help you with answers during this step.

Ask someone to read Revelation 2:12, 13.

How does Jesus describe Himself here? (The one who has the double-edged sword.)

Why do you think He uses these words? (It may reinforce the point that Jesus is in control. Jesus will ultimately judge the church's enemies. But also check out Hebrews 4:12. The Word of God is compared to a "double-edged sword." Jesus wields the powerful and true words of God.)

What does Jesus "know"? (Where they live. The situation in Pergamum, how difficult things are for them.)

Let's get some background. Pergamum was another major city, on a par with Smyrna, not as big as Ephesus. It was a religious center. Half a dozen religions had important shrines there. It was in Pergamum that the first temple was built to a Roman emperor (Augustus) about a century before this was written. This is probably "Satan's throne" that was mentioned here.

Apparently, as in Smyrna, there was persecution happening here. We know nothing else about this Antipas, except that he was martyred for his faith—probably for refusing to offer a sacrifice to the emperor.

Ask someone to read verses 14 and 15.

What were they doing wrong? (Tolerating those who followed Balaam's teaching and the Nicolaitans.)

Does anyone remember who Balaam was? (Some may remember the talking donkey incident, but they probably won't recall the context.)

Here's the story, from Numbers 22-24. Balaam was a prophet who was hired by a rival king (Balak) to utter a curse on the Israelites. God would not let him do this (making the donkey talk back to him). But Balaam advised the king to send women to seduce the Israelite men. These women drew these men into the worship of false gods, and that meant disaster for the Israelites.

Now that you know this about Balaam, what do you think was going on in Pergamum? (Several religions of the area involved sexual rites and temple prostitution. Apparently, some of these people were infiltrating the church and leading some Christians into sexual immorality and false religions.)

What's this business about food sacrificed to idols? In Romans and I Corinthians it seemed that Paul took a pretty lax position on this issue. Why is it such a problem here? (Apparently Christians were being drawn into pagan cults by participating in their feasts. Earlier, Paul had indicated that the eating of the food itself was no big deal—but even then he acknowledged that some weaker believers might find the temptation too great and should avoid these feasts altogether.)

Who were the Nicolaitans? (We don't know. Apparently they were heretical teachers who had infiltrated the church. Interestingly, the term is related to the name of Balaam. Balaam in Hebrew means "conquer the people." Nicolaos in Greek means the same thing. It can also mean "victory people" and this may give us a clue. They may have been "Christians" who claimed total freedom from any behavior restrictions—claiming "victory" over the law. If so, they might be related to those John alludes to in I John 1:6, 8, 10, who "say they have no sin." Revelation may be implying that the "victory people" are in a position to be seduced by the Balaam-like "people-conquerors" of the pagan cults.)

Ask someone to read verse 16.

Ask: **What were the people supposed to do?** (Repent!)

How might they do that? (Recommitting themselves to God's truth; excommunicating those who teach things contrary to God's truth, etc.)

What does Jesus threaten to do? (Come and get rid of the false teachers Himself.)

There's that sword again. What's that about? (The sword *of [His] mouth* is almost definitely His powerful word of judgment.)

3
The Nicolaitan Network

(10 minutes)

Poking Fun at the Excesses of False Religion

Have a group member, male or female, prepared to do a dramatic reading of Resource 10, "The Power of the Air." (This would be especially good to put on video and play for the group, if you have the equipment.)

After the skit, talk about it. **Naturally, this was exaggerated. But were there any things that especially hit home? Are churches in danger of going in this direction?**

If the conversation doesn't get going right away, try prompting it with these questions. [Note: You won't have time to deal fully with all these questions. Use a few to get discussion started.)

What do you think of the church's motto, "Love, love, love, whatever that means"? Do some Christians really follow that philosophy? (Love *is* at the core of Christian faith, but some Christians don't pay much attention to the scriptural "nuts and bolts" on *how* to love.)

The host said something like, "I can't presume to tell you what to believe." Is there some validity in that? When does it go too far? (To a point, each person needs to make individual decisions about spiritual things, yet a Christian should be able to say with some certainty what he or she believes. It goes too far when it assumes that the realities of God and the universe are different for every person.)

What about this "Rahab" singer? Do you think Christians use come-ons that are too worldly? Are we too obsessed with "famous" Christian performers and authors? Do we latch too quickly onto famous people who become Christians and "use" them?

Do you think that a lot of Christians are swayed by the idea that "there are many roads to the top of the mountain"? How can

we present the exclusivity of Jesus without seeming totally obnoxious? (People want to believe that all religions are true. But there's a huge problem of logic there. If the Muslim is right in his or her beliefs, for example, then the Christian is wrong and vice versa. You have a right to believe that all systems are somehow valid, but that's not Christianity. The Bible makes clear that Jesus is the only way. It also makes clear that God wants everyone to be saved and offers Jesus to everyone.)

How could these false teachings act as a wet blanket on your spiritual fire? (By keeping you from "offending" others with the idea that Jesus is the only way to heaven; by living a secondhand spiritual life through the exploits of Christian celebrities, etc.)

4
Bible Drill
(10 minutes)

Using God's Sword to Oppose Falsehood

Twice in our text, the Lord talks about His "sword." It seems clear that He's talking about His Word. This is the way to oppose false teaching—by grounding ourselves in Scripture.

So we're going to finish up with a game that involves the Bible. But I hope it's more than a game. It might encourage you to keep examining the ideas and philosophies you come across, in the light of the Bible.

For this game you'll need to dig out Resource 9, the true-false test. I'll give you a separate sheet with Bible passages listed. Each of the passages helps to answer one of those statements on the true-false test. In the space next to the Scripture reference, write the number of the statement to which it applies.

Divide into teams. Here are the rules. Everyone in each group must be working on the same text at the same time. Look up the passage, have someone read it aloud, and decide together which statement it applies to. The first group to give me a correctly completed form is the winner.

What do you win? A gift certificate for Rahab's latest album!

Give a copy of Resource 11, "Scripture List," to each team. When teams have finished, go through the Scriptures and the statements if time allows. If not, close in prayer—asking God for wisdom in applying His Word to the teachings you run across.

If you'd like to prepare people for next time, hand out copies of Resource 12, "Destination: Thyatira." Encourage group members to work through it, using any Bible study helps they may have as well as Scripture itself.

Answers
6	A.	Isaiah 47:13, 14
10	B.	Luke 12:19-21
1	C.	John 3:18
3	D.	Acts 4:12
4	E.	I Thessalonians 4:13, 14
8	F.	II Timothy 1:9
7	G.	II Timothy 3:16
2	H.	Hebrews 9:27
5	I.	Hebrews 13:4
9	J.	I John 3:17

WHAT DO YOU THINK?

In Column A, put T or F, according to whether you think each statement's true or false.

In Column B, put T or F, according to whether most of the people you know think each statement's true or false.

What You Think A	What Others Think B
____	____
____	____
____	____
____	____
____	____
____	____
____	____
____	____
____	____
____	____

1. It doesn't matter what you believe, as long as you're nice to people.

2. If you do good in this life, you will be reincarnated as a good person in the next.

3. Belief in Jesus is the only way to get to heaven.

4. After you die, there's nothing else.

5. Sexual relations should be reserved for marriage.

6. Astrology can help guide your life.

7. The Bible is God's Word.

8. If you're good in this life, you'll go to heaven.

9. God wants us to share our wealth with those in need.

10. The most important thing in life is to have a good time.

THE POWER OF THE AIR

HOST: Greetings, friends! And welcome to the Church of the Power of the Air, where our motto is: "Love, love, love, whatever that means."

We have a full slate of activities on our show—I mean, in our *service*—today. You'll get a real kick out of—I mean, *blessing*! You'll get a real *blessing* out of the service today. And that's what it's all about, isn't it?

Well, that's what it's all about for *me*, anyway. I wouldn't presume to say what it's all about for *you*. Whatever turns you on.

And I'm glad you turned *us* on, because you are going to love our special awareness-raising emphasis today. We have endangered oat bran, we have recycling UFOs—and we have that singing sensation, Rahab!

That's right. Later in the show, she'll be doing her smash hit, "Please Me, Tease Me," except she's changing the words to "Preach Me, Teach Me." She's changed the words, but she still has all the moves you guys love so well.

But first, let me offer the devotional of the day. Let's see—we haven't tried the Bible in a while. Let me pick a text at random. (*Opens Bible randomly.*)

There. The Gospel of John, chapter 14, verse 6. "Jesus answered, 'I am the way and the truth and the life . . . .'" Obviously, what He means here is that there are many roads to the top of the mountain.

He goes on: ". . . No one comes to the Father except through me." Right. What He meant to say was, "through Me in the many different forms I take." Believe whatever you want; just be cool about it, okay?

Let's try another verse. (*Opens Bible again.*) The Acts of the Apostles, chapter 4, verse 12. "Salvation is found in no one else. For there is no other name under heaven given to men by which we must be saved." You see, that's what I don't like about the Bible. It's so hard to understand. Like this, for instance.

(*Opens Bible again.*) The Book of Hebrews. Let's try that 4:12 thing again. "For the word of God is living and active. Sharper than any double-edged sword, it penetrates even to dividing soul and spirit, joints and marrow; it judges the thoughts and attitudes of the heart."

Right. Well, what this really means is . . . is . . . Well, let's listen to that smash hit from recording star Rahab—"Please Me . . . " I mean, "Preach Me, Teach Me." All right? All right!

(*Sits back, exhausted, then plunges into the Bible again, saying to self:*) Does it really say that?

Scripture List

RESOURCE 11

_____ **A. Isaiah 47:13, 14**

_____ **B. Luke 12:19-21**

_____ **C. John 3:18**

_____ **D. Acts 4:12**

_____ **E. I Thessalonians 4:13, 14**

_____ **F. II Timothy 1:9**

_____ **G. II Timothy 3:16**

_____ **H. Hebrews 9:27**

_____ **I. Hebrews 13:4**

_____ **J. I John 3:17**

DESTINATION: THYATIRA

From a Commentary or Study Bible
Background on Thyatira:

From the text (Revelation 2:18-29)
How does Christ describe Himself?

What does He "know"?

Course of action:

JUST SAY NO
Learning from the Church at Thyatira

We've all heard the high-profile stories of how sex can lure Christians from the "straight and narrow"—televangelists falling into disgrace after liaisons in motel rooms, pastors forced to resign after admitting affairs.

But what about average Christians? What about the man whose pornography addiction builds a wall between himself and the Lord? What about the woman whose fantasies about TV stars keep her mind wandering when she could be meditating on Scripture?

The world is only too ready to snuff out our spiritual fire with sexual distractions. Many of us are only too ready to give in.

This session will help your group discuss and deal with the way sexual temptation can draw us away from Christ. As you'll see, it's a session the church at Thyatira could have used, too.

A word about our title: "Just say no" is appropriate because it takes discipline to remain holy in a sex-crazy world. But too often, Christian teaching about sex has stopped with, "Say no! Deny that you are a sexual being!" The world has rightly questioned that approach.

The fact is that we say yes to holiness, to fully committed love, to humanity as it was meant to be, when we say no to casual sex. That's the message that needs to be heard in your group.

Where You're Headed:
To help group members consider how sexual sin pulls people away from following Christ, and to help them arm themselves against sexual temptation.

Scriptures You'll Apply:
Revelation 2:18-29

Things You'll Need:
• Bibles
• Pens or pencils
• Copies of "Fancy Meeting You Here" (Resource 13) for two actresses who are prepared to read it
• Copies of "Action Sheet" (Resource 14)
• Copies of Resource 15, "Destination: Sardis" (optional)

1
Our Sex-Crazy Age
(10 minutes)

Evaluating What Our
World Thinks about Sex

Let's say, for the next couple of minutes, that you're not a Christian. You believe pretty much what most people in our society believe about sex. I'm going to interview you about your opinions on the following subjects. Give me your answers in a sentence or two.

Is sex good or bad? (Good.)

Under what circumstances? (Some would say, "Any." Others, "With someone you love.")

Which would you rather have: spirituality, kindness, or sex appeal? (Sex appeal scores very high.)

How are love and sex related? (Some would say love is irrelevant, but many would say sex should be an expression of love. They may, however, be using the term "love" loosely.)

What do you think about safe sex? (Unfortunately, a necessity.)

Virginity? (Out of date. Get rid of it.)

Extramarital affairs? (Awful if someone gets hurt, but understandable in many circumstances.)

Divorce? (An unfortunate fact of life. Just get—or keep—all the money you can.)

Prostitution? (Tacky, disease-ridden, but not too bad for those who want it; a victimless crime.)

Pornography? (Tacky, but not too bad if you keep it away from the kids; if you don't like it, don't look at it—but don't ban it.)

Living together before marriage? (Can be a good way to get to know each other.)

Now go back over the list of topics and ask: **Now, speaking as yourself, what is the Christian view on each of these issues?**

You can deal with the specific issues you've listed, but this overview may help you:

Sexual intimacy is a special gift that God intends for married couples to enjoy. It *is* an expression of love, but it is a supreme expression of *serious* love, the kind of love that results in life-long commitment. It is an expression of *unity*, a unity between two people that mirrors the unity of God.

Any sexual intimacy apart from that life-long commitment is "faking it." It is less than what God intends. It is misusing His special gift.

Sexuality is part of who we are, the way God made us. But it's just a part. The Bible warns against overemphasizing physical pleasure and ignoring our spiritual side.

What could happen to a Christian who absorbed the world's views of sexuality and started acting on them?

What effect could it have on his or her relationship with Christ?

Let's look at an example in the Book of Revelation.

2
Dyeing to Be in Thyatira
(5 minutes)

Getting Some Background on the City and the Church

If you passed out copies of Resource 12, "Destination: Thyatira," last time, ask any who filled them out to help you with answers during the next couple of steps.

Thyatira was about forty miles inland from Pergamum. It was not a major city, not nearly as large as the three we've discussed already. But it was a center for labor guilds and craftspeople.

We know of one biblical character who came from Thyatira. Ask someone to read Acts 16:13, 14. **Lydia was a businesswoman from this city. It's not surprising that she sold purple cloth, since Thyatira was known for its dyeing capabilities, among other trades.**

The trade unions and guilds would have had patron gods they worshiped. They would have had regular feast days for these gods (anything for a day off!). These holidays may have involved sexual escapades as well.

3
The Jezebel Story
(18 minutes)

Examining the Biblical Text

Ask someone to read Revelation 2:18, 19.

How does Jesus describe Himself? (Son of God, eyes of blazing fire, feet of burnished bronze.)

Why do you think He uses these terms? What would this have meant to the craftspeople of Thyatira? (The terms would probably have gotten the attention of the smiths, who worked with iron and bronze—and with fire. Anyone familiar with the Old Testament would be reminded of Daniel's descriptions of beings he saw in visions [see Daniel 10:6]. These beings predicted the future and pronounced judgment. Jesus makes it clear: He means business.)

What does Jesus "know"? What's good about the Thyatira church? (Their deeds, their love and faith, their service and perseverance, and the increase in their faithfulness since the beginning.)

How do you think the people in the church would have felt after hearing that? (Pretty good.)

What kind of "deeds" do you think they were doing? What kind of "service" were they involved in? (Probably acts of caring for the poor, worshiping God, sharing their faith.)

Why do you think they had to "persevere"? (As with the other churches, there was persecution. The trick was to share your faith without being too open about it. The actual arrests and sentencing were mostly in the hands of local governors. If you didn't make waves, they could ignore you. But this church was apparently growing—at least in activity. It may have had to weather some crackdowns.)

Ask someone to read verse 20.

So what's the problem in Thyatira? (Jezebel.)

What do we know about her?

(1. "You tolerate" probably means that she was in the church.

2. She called herself a prophetess—like others in churches of that time.

3. She was teaching in the church.

4. She was leading Christians into sexual immorality.

5. She was leading Christians into involvement with false religions—participation in the feasts of the gods. The word "servants" here may indicate that Christian leaders were being led astray.)

Why do you think the prophetess is called "Jezebel"? (In the Old Testament, Jezebel was a wicked queen who lured the Israelites into the worship of the false god Baal.)

If you have time, make the following points:

There were other prophets in churches of that time. They regularly spoke out with special words of direction and encouragement from God (Acts 11:27-30). Both men and women had this gift (Acts 2:17; 21:9). So the problem was not that this woman was prophesying. It was in what she was saying.

How could the church let itself believe that sexual immorality was okay? For one thing, many ancient religions used sex in the worship of their gods. For another, the church was still figuring out what Christianity was. And third, not everyone understood that being free from the law didn't mean throwing out sexual restrictions.

If you were a pastor in Thyatira and some prophetess slithered into your office saying, "Hey, God has shown me a great new way to worship," it might be difficult to say no.

Ask someone to read verses 21-23.

How did Christ deal with this false prophetess? (Gave her time to repent, then would bring suffering on her and her followers.)

How did the punishment fit the crime? (She had sinned on a bed of adultery; she would be punished on a sickbed.)

Why do you think the punishment seems so severe? (Probably because it was within the church. Especially in that first century, it was crucial that the church keep its course. Judgment was often harsh—see Acts 5:1-11.)

Ask someone to read verses 24, 25.

What does Christ say to those in the church who had not been led astray? ("Hold on to what you have.")

What did they have? (A holy relationship with Christ; loving relationships with each other; perhaps good marriages; God's Word.)

Note: Someone may ask what the "so-called deep secrets of Satan" were. We're not sure. There are several theories, but they're not worth getting into. Most likely, Jezebel was promising a fuller experience of spirituality through the "deep secrets" of God. But Christ says here that they're not God's deep secrets, but Satan's.

4
Two Women
(12 minutes)

Drawing Examples from
Biblical Characters

Have two women from the group present the drama from Resource 13, "Fancy Meeting You Here." Introduce it by saying, **This is merely conjecture, of course. But what would have happened if Lydia, now an older woman, came back to her hometown and encountered Jezebel? It might have gone something like this.**

After the drama, ask a few questions. **What were Jezebel's reasons for doing what she did? How are these like modern-day reasons?**

How did Lydia respond? Were there other responses she could have given?

As needed, add the following information to the discussion:

Jezebel raised several issues, first of *power*. **Sex, she claimed, was an area in which women have power. That claim has been made in modern times; but only Christianity, rightly applied, is an empowerer of all, men and women alike.**

She also claimed that people are essentially sexual beings, and they need the freedom to express that. Lydia countered by saying that people are not *just* **sexual beings. Without self-control, they tend to become merely sexual—which dehumanizes them.**

Jezebel claimed that sex somehow put her *in touch with divine power*. **This, too, is claimed today, especially in New Age contexts. Lydia argued that those "forces" Jezebel was in touch with were ultimately destructive. We "touch" God through Jesus.**

Jezebel wanted "more" than Christianity, but Lydia said she was settling for less. Modern cults (and permissiveness in general) make great promises, but what we have as Christians is better than what they are offering.

5
Holding On
(10 minutes)

Finding Practical Ways to
Hang on to Sexual Purity

Do you agree or disagree with the following statement: "In our culture, sex is like a religion"? Why?

Let people debate this for a minute or so. Note that on TV and in the movies, people "sing the praises" of sex. There are "high priests" and "priestesses" who lead the crowd. People are constantly studying how to do better at it.

This religion of sex, like Jezebel, entices us. It promises us ultimate satisfaction, but it doesn't deliver. Still, it makes us want. The strategy of this religion is to make us unhappy with what we have, to want more.

The message of Revelation is important to us. "Hold on to what you have." What we have as Christians is better than what others are promising.

How do we convince ourselves of that?

Hand out Resource 14, "Action Sheet." **Here are some suggestions. Look over these. Pick out one that you can do, beginning this week. Check off at least one, maybe two or three.**

If none of these appeal to you, make up your own strategy in

the "Other" line. In each case, fill in the details of your situation. Let's look over it.

"Stop watching certain TV shows or movies that encourage lust." Naturally, what we take in affects the way we think and act.

"Recognize sex-oriented ads and say no to them." When you see an ad that uses sex to make you want something, put your guard up. Say, "This isn't going to work with me."

"Get out of an unhealthy sexual relationship." Easier said than done. But if you're in one, rely on God's strength to take the necessary steps to get out of it. Get help if you need it.

"Communicate better with my spouse on sexual matters." Many of us find it hard to talk about sex with each other, but it's important that sex within marriage be as mutually pleasing as possible. Sex is a holy expression of marital love.

"Recommit myself to my marriage." Maybe you need to shut the door to the idea of extramarital affairs by saying yes to your spouse all over again.

"Discipline my mind to keep from dwelling on sexual thoughts." Replace distracting thoughts with thoughts about God. Memorize Bible verses. Pray for those in need.

"Spend an extra five minutes a day this week in prayer, devoting my sexuality to God." Sex is God's gift, whether you're single or married. He cares about what we do with it.

"Stay away from people who steer me toward sexual immorality." Is anyone encouraging you to let down your guard in this area? Is he or she having a greater influence on you than you are on him or her?

Ask group members to keep this paper during the week, using it to check their progress.

Close in prayer, asking God for strength in withstanding the sexual temptation of this world.

If you'd like to prepare people for next time, hand out copies of Resource 15, "Destination: Sardis." Encourage group members to work through it, using any Bible study helps they may have as well as Scripture itself.

FANCY MEETING YOU HERE

JEZEBEL: Well, if it isn't Lydia. I thought you retired to your villa in Philippi.

LYDIA: I did. Timothy and John sent for me. They said there were some problems here in Thyatira.

JEZEBEL: They meant me.

LYDIA: If you're the one they call "Jezebel."

JEZEBEL: I'm afraid I am. Those men, they just don't understand, do they?

LYDIA: Understand what?

JEZEBEL: Us. You and me. Women. They play their church game and get really upset when a female tries to barge in.

LYDIA: Oh, really?

JEZEBEL: Look at them. Timothy, John, Mark, Clement, old Silas—

LYDIA: Phoebe, Priscilla, Euodias . . . Lydia.

JEZEBEL: Yeah, yeah. Still, men have the power. But I've found a turf where I can beat them. It's what we have and they want. Sex is where our power is.

LYDIA: Our power is in Jesus Christ.

JEZEBEL: I knew you would say that. I do believe in Jesus—I really do. He opened the way for us, out of that awful legal system. He set us free to enjoy who we are—sexual beings.

LYDIA: Is that all we are?

JEZEBEL: Isn't that enough? We can share in the divine power, Lydia. Through sex, we can feast in the presence of God.

LYDIA: Which temple did you get that from? Apollo? No, he's male. Artemis, maybe? Isis? Or Cybele, the Great Mother?

JEZEBEL: Does it matter? They are all one with the God you worship. There are forces out there calling us to be free from senseless restrictions, to experience the joys of physical pleasure.

LYDIA: To gorge ourselves at the feasts of the gods until we can't walk anymore? To use the sacred gift of our sexuality with people we don't even know? That's life as it was meant to be?

JEZEBEL: Oh, what do you know about it?

LYDIA: I tried those temples as a young woman. I thought they would free me, but they left me empty. In Philippi I used to go down to the river and call out to any god who might hear me. One day a man came to the river and told me about Jesus. Jesus freed me to be me.

JEZEBEL: That's fine for you, but I need more.

LYDIA: More? Then why are you settling for so much less? Are you only a bundle of bones and impulses in some pretty skin? When that skin wrinkles, when you're as old as I am, will you still be free? Or will you be a slave to your own body?

JEZEBEL: I knew you wouldn't understand.

LYDIA: Oh, but I do. Those "forces" out there are lying to you. Say no to them before it's too late.

JEZEBEL: Nice try, Lydia. But it's not working. I've made my bed; I'm going to keep lying in it.

LYDIA: God have mercy on you. If you change your mind, come see me in Philippi. I have a nice place there—down by the river.

ACTION SHEET

Stop watching certain TV shows or movies that encourage lust.

☞ What shows?

Recognize sex-oriented ads and say no to them.

☞ List ads as you spot them:

Get out of an unhealthy sexual relationship.

☞ How? When?

Communicate better with my spouse on sexual matters.

☞ How? When?

Recommit myself to my marriage.

☞ How? When?

Discipline my mind to keep from dwelling on sexual thoughts.

☞ What to think of instead:

Spend an extra five minutes a day this week in prayer, devoting my sexuality to God.

☞ Check off each day: **M T W T F S S**

Stay away from people who steer me toward sexual immorality.

☞ Who?

Other ideas:

☞ Specifics?

DESTINATION: SARDIS

RESOURCE
15

WELCOME TO
SARDIS
the Sleepy City

From a Commentary or Study Bible
Background on Sardis:

From the text (Revelation 3:1-6)
How does Christ describe Himself?

What does He "know"?

Course of action:

DEAD FAITH
Learning from the Church at Sardis

Every so often, the "faith vs. works" debate crops up again. It's Paul vs. James, Martin Luther vs. St. Francis, libertine vs. legalist.

Naturally, faith and works go together. It's possible, however, to fall off one side or the other. "Faith without works is dead," said James. Paul spent a couple of epistles saying, in essence, "Works without faith are dead."

The Lord says to the church at Sardis, "Faith without works is *incomplete*."

A living faith in Jesus Christ opens the door to the Holy Spirit, who gives you the power to do good things. If I invest in a new computer, buying it is only the beginning. If I never plug it in and use it, my computer experience is incomplete.

Paul has a great turn of phrase in Ephesians 2. After assuring us that we are saved by God's grace, not works, he says, "We are God's workmanship, created in Christ Jesus to do good works, which God prepared in advance for us to do." God has invested in us! And He wants to plug us in and switch us on.

Like too many Christians, those at Sardis were basking in old glory. Their faith was something that got them into the fold a long time ago, but didn't make much difference in their lives.

Christ's message to us is His message to Sardis: "Wake up!"

Where You're Headed:
To wake your group members up, to challenge them to put their faith into action.

Scriptures You'll Apply:
Revelation 3:1-6

Things You'll Need:
• Bibles
• Pens or pencils
• Copies of "The Church of the Blessed Memory" (Resource 16) for five actors only
• Copies of "Plotting for Growth" (Resource 17)
• Index cards
• Group members prepared to do the skit on Resource 16
• Copies of Resource 18, "Destination: Philadelphia" (optional)

1
Glory Days

Remembering Our Past
and How We've Changed

Hand an index card to each group member. Ask people to choose a year in the past: If they're 50 or older, they should think back 20 years; if they're 30-50, think back 10 years; under that, think back 5 years.

I want you to write down one of your greatest accomplishments of that year (and it's okay if you cheat by a year or two). But don't make it too personal, because we will be sharing these.

Give each person a few minutes to think of something and fill out the card. Then collect the cards. Go through them one by one, reading each accomplishment and seeing whether the group can guess who did it. Have fun with this.

Then say something like this: **We've been talking about things we did years ago, but we've all done a lot of things since. What if we hadn't? What if that were the last important thing we'd done?**

You may know people like that—maybe a high school quarterback who keeps telling you about his championship season. There's something very sad about that.

How do some Christians do the same thing spiritually? (They made a decision for Christ when they were 10, or 15, or 30, and that's the last important thing they've done. They show up at church, they're glad to be saved, but they haven't been letting the Lord do things in their lives since.)

We'll be looking at a church like that today.

2
Home Is Where It's Sardis
(8 minutes)

Getting Some Background
on the Ancient City

If you passed out copies of Resource 15, "Destination: Sardis," last time, ask any who filled them out to help you with answers during the next couple of steps.

The fifth church of Revelation was located in Sardis, about 30 miles south of Thyatira. Sardis had seen its day. It had a great history, but it was going downhill.

You may have heard of King Croesus, who was fabulously wealthy. Sardis was his capital. It was at a major crossroads. It had a strong fortress. It had a lot going for it. But then it was conquered by the Persians, and later by the Greeks.

By Roman times, Sardis was playing second fiddle to the major cities on the coast—Ephesus and Smyrna. An earthquake hit it in A.D. 17, and it never really recovered.

A few details you should know:
• The town had begun building a massive temple to the goddess Artemis. It would have been as great as the one at Ephesus—but construction was never completed.

• In the distance, on the skyline, the people of Sardis could see a massive cemetery—thousands of burial mounds. The city seemed to have a preoccupation with death.

• There was a substantial wool industry based in Sardis. This may explain the references to clothing in the passage we'll look at. Some might even suggest that the people took on the lethargic attitude of the sheep they tended.

3
Wake-Up Call

(20 minutes)

Learning from
Sardis's Mistakes

Ask someone to read Revelation 3:1.

How does Jesus describe Himself? (The one who holds the seven spirits and seven stars.)

What does this mean? (Once again, Jesus is in control. Don't worry too much about what the spirits and stars represent.)

What does He "know"? (Their deeds—both in reputation and reality. The word for reputation is literally "name." He says, in effect, "You are famous for being alive, but you're really dead." We know from history that this was true of the city. We shall see it was also true of the church.)

Ask someone to read verse 2.

What did the people need to do? (Wake up! Strengthen what remains.)

In what way do you think they were "asleep"? (Perhaps not caring about their faith, not growing in the Lord, not paying attention to the needs of society around them, etc.)

What are the things that "remain"—which they needed to strengthen? (Perhaps the amount of faith they have, their fellowship, their commitment to obeying Christ.)

Why do you think their deeds were not "complete"? (They were not "following through" on their faith. They had apparently taken the first few steps of Christianity, but they hadn't let God lead them into full obedience. They were Christians in name only.)

Ask someone to read verse 3.

What did Christ want them to do? (Remember, obey, and repent.)

What had they "received and heard"? (The message of the Gospel; the teaching of the apostles.)

What would happen if they didn't wake up? (He would come suddenly, like a thief, to judge them. This may be a reference to the Second Coming, but it may just refer to the suddenness of losing things. You "wake up" one day and say, "It used to feel good to be a Christian, but now it doesn't. God seemed to be with me a moment ago, but now He seems far away.")

Ask someone to read verses 4-6.

What do you think the white clothing would mean to those in the textile industry of Sardis? (It would be a powerful symbol of something pure, something good. In those days, as today, one could be turned away from a feast if his clothing was soiled.)

Those who had "soiled their clothes"—how do you think they had done this? (Probably by compromising with the culture, by joining in emperor-worship or cult worship.)

Looking back over this passage, what's missing? There's an element from some other passages that we don't find here. What is that? (Persecution. There is no mention of them undergoing persecution for their faith.)

Why do you think this is? (It's possible that the local authorities didn't care. But it's more likely that the Christians went with the flow—offering incense to the emperor just to fit in, taking part in the pagan feasts to be "good citizens.")

What is promised to those who "overcome"? (They will be

dressed in white; their names stay in the Book of Life.)

You may want to mention that the name-erasing probably refers to a custom in many ancient cities of keeping a roll book of citizens. When a citizen died—or was convicted of a major crime—his or her name was erased. It is possible that some "unsoiled" believers had been convicted for their Christianity and their names had been erased from the town book. Even if this is not the case, it is something wishy-washy believers would have feared. Christ promises that those who honor Him will be in His book forever.

The Lord is saying, in effect, "You're so interested in being good citizens, why not be a citizen of *My* kingdom? Whose side are you on?"

After studying this passage, what impression do you have of the church at Sardis?

Do you know Christians like that today?

Think about this: To what extent does that describe you?

4
Once Upon a Time
(8 minutes)

Taking a Humorous Look at Dusty Spirituality

Have several group members present the skit from Resource 16, "The Church of the Blessed Memory."

Afterward, talk about it.

Why was that so frustrating for the leader? (He wanted to move forward, but everyone else was reliving the past.)

If you could get those people to do one thing to jump-start their spiritual lives, what would it be?

5
Plotting for Growth
(8 minutes)

Evaluating Our Spiritual Progress and Planning Ways to Step Forward

Hand out Resource 17, "Plotting for Growth."

Each of us has a different story. We're supposed to be growing in Christ, but some of us may have gotten stuck. Maybe there was a moment—on a hilltop, or at a festival—when we got close to God, but it's been downhill ever since.

Use this graph to plot your spiritual growth over the course of your life. There are five sections to this graph. Whatever your age is, divide it by five. Each section represents that many years.

This is only for you, so be honest. How spiritually "on fire" have you been at these points?

How close to God have you been?

After you have completed the graph, there are some tough questions to think about and answer.

Give group members several minutes to complete the Resource sheet.

Discuss it as appropriate and as time allows, perhaps one on one. Offer to meet afterward with anyone who wants advice or prayer.

Close in prayer, asking God to wake you all up and keep you awake as you seek to be faithful to Him.

If you'd like to prepare people for next time, hand out copies of Resource 18, "Destination: Philadephia." Encourage group members to work through it, using any Bible study helps they may have as well as Scripture itself.

THE CHURCH OF THE BLESSED MEMORY

(RALPH arrives at church, where the others are milling around.)

WALTER *(greeting him with a handshake):* Welcome, sir. Haven't I seen you somewhere before?

RALPH: I don't think so. This is my first time here. I'm a friend of the pastor. I'm supposed to lead a Bible study.

WALTER: Well, you're in the right place—The Church of the Blessed Memory. But let me tell you, you're a dead ringer for a pastor we used to have here, years ago. Great preacher, greatest I ever heard. What was his name? *(calling to wife)* Effie!

EFFIE: Yes, Walter?

WALTER: That's it. Walter. No, that's my name. But don't you worry. I'll think of it. Great preacher, that one. *(He shuffles off.)*

EFFIE *(coming over):* Don't mind him. That's just my husband, Walter. *(Taps her head)* Mind like an open canyon. We had a beautiful wedding, though. 1935. I was all in white. I remember gazing at him as he said, "I do." He hasn't spoken a word of sense since.

RALPH *(summoning others to sit down):* Well, I thought maybe we could get started. I'm Ralph Sparks, your Bible study leader while Pastor Joe is on vacation.

VELMA: He's in the Smokey Mountains.

RALPH: Yes, he is.

VELMA: It's beautiful there. One Sunday I was visiting there and went up on a hilltop to pray. It was so peaceful. I'll never forget it.

RALPH: Thank you for sharing that. Our text today is Revelation 3:1-6. Would you like to read that for us?

VELMA: Love to. But instead, let me read my favorite psalm—Psalm 23. That's what I read up on that mountain. If you don't mind, I'd like to read it my own special way. "The. The Lord. The Lord is. The Lord is my. . . ."

EFFIE: For goodness sake, Velma, you've been reading it that way for three years. It sounds like a football cheer.

TARA: I was a cheerleader three years ago, in high school! Gimme a G!

RALPH: Wait a second. I think we're getting a little out of hand.

WALTER: You know, that's just what what's-his-name used to say. What *was* his name?

RALPH: Velma—

WALTER: No, it wasn't Velma.

RALPH: I mean, Velma, would you like to read the text?

VELMA: Thank you. *(clears throat)* "The. The Lord. . . ."

(CONTINUED)

THE CHURCH OF THE BLESSED MEMORY (CONT.)

RALPH: No, I mean the text from Revelation.

TARA: Oh, I love Revelation. All that prophecy. That's what they talked about at End Times '89. You know, that big festival? It was awesome.

RALPH: Thank you. Maybe *you* could read the Scripture for us.

TARA: I'd love to, but, like, I don't have a Bible. I mean, I have a Bible at home, but it's full of autographs I got at End Times '89. I even got one from Paul.

RALPH: Paul?

WALTER: No, that wasn't his name either.

TARA: No, Paul from that group back in the 40s—Peter, Paul, and Marcy, I think.

RALPH: I see. But why come to a Bible study without a Bible?

TARA: Because we've been doing Psalm 23 for as long as I can remember. I know it by heart now.

TARA and VELMA: "The! The Lord! The Lord is. . . ."

RALPH: Stop it! Please! I'm getting really harried.

WALTER: That was his name. Harry.

EFFIE: He was the one who married us. Walter was such a beautiful groom. And now look.

RALPH: If I could just have some order here, we could begin. Good. Our text for today is . . . (*He stops and, with a sigh, decides to give in.*) the Twenty-Third Psalm. We'll read it in unison.

ALL: "The. The Lord. The Lord is. . . ."

PLOTTING FOR GROWTH

RESOURCE
17

SPIRITUAL GROWTH CHART

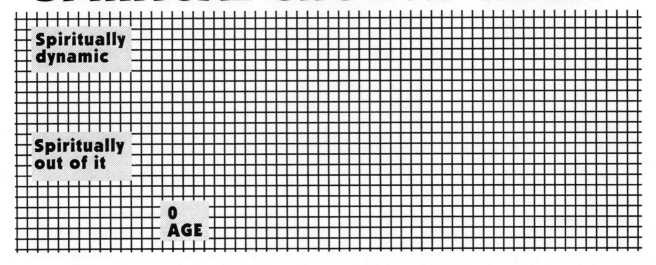

Spiritually
dynamic

Spiritually
out of it

0
AGE

The Christians at Sardis seemed to be making compromises in order to fit into their society. Have you been doing the same thing? What compromises have you been making . . .

    . . . in the area of money?

    . . . in the area of sexual behavior?

    . . . in the area of work ethics?

    . . . in the area of social interactions?

    . . . in other areas?

What can you do this week to stop making those compromises?

If the graph above is going steadily uphill, great. What habits can you adopt to assure that you'll *stay* awake and keep growing?

If the graph has plateaued, what can you do to spark new growth?

If it's going downhill, what can you do *this week* to stop the slide?

Christ told the Sardians to "strengthen what remains." If you're a "downhill racer" right now, what aspects of your spiritual life do remain? How can you build on these?

DESTINATION: PHILADELPHIA

From a Commentary or Study Bible
Background on Philadelphia:

From the text (Revelation 3:7-13)
How does Christ describe Himself?

What does He "know"?

Course of action:

HERE COMES THE SON
Learning from the Church at Philadelphia

Jesus is coming back!

We forget that so easily. We go about our daily lives as if this world were all that mattered. But Jesus is coming back!

He will make all things new. The injustices of our present world will be history, because Jesus will be fully in charge. He will reward His faithful servants with smiles of delight. We will bask in His love and feast on His joy.

That promise should pull us forward through life. It should draw us like a magnet toward God's kingdom. It should give us the energy to live each day.

"What did this day mean in terms of the kingdom?" we should be asking ourselves. "Will these activities be important as I look back from an eternal perspective?"

That perspective changes the way we think about material things, about other people, about time and effort. "Seek first the kingdom of God," Jesus said in effect, "and all these things will come as well."

The church you'll study in this session got nothing but praise from the Lord. Its members were going through difficult trials, but Jesus put it in perspective for them: "I am coming soon!" That should clear things up for us as well.

Where You're Headed:
To remind group members that Jesus is returning, and to explore how that assurance should affect our lives.

Scriptures You'll Apply:
Revelation 3:7-13

Things You'll Need:
- Bibles
- Pens or pencils
- A copy of "Role-ing in Dough" (Resource 19) cut into three parts
- Copies of "Because He's Coming Back" (Resource 20)
- Copies of Resource 21, "Destination: Laodicea" (optional)

1
Open-Door Policy

(8 minutes)

Playing with the Image
of the "Open Door"

Start with the following imagination game.

You're in a horror film. You're being chased by the Monster from Beyond the Deep. You're running down a hallway. It seems endless. The monster is behind you, gaining on you. You feel its hot, sticky breath on your back. Suddenly you see an open door ahead of you.

What does that open door mean to you? (Safety; a place to rest; maybe you'll get out of this after all.)

Now imagine this. A rich friend invites you to spend a weekend at his luxurious mansion in the country. You drive to this splendid house, and as you approach the front door, a butler appears and opens it for you. He greets you by name and says, "It's good to have you with us. Please make yourself at home."

What does that open door mean to you? (Access to a great weekend; nothing but pleasure for a couple of days.)

You are a door-to-door salesperson. You have been traipsing through this neighborhood all day, getting doors slammed in your face. No sales. Not even a kind word. At one home, however, the door swings open and the homeowner says, "Come on in, have a seat."

What does that open door mean to you? (A kindness; an opportunity to sell your product; a place to rest.)

You have just bought your first home. You have packed up the moving van and driven across the country to your new address. You pull into the driveway, walk up to the door, insert your shiny gold key and . . . it doesn't open. You push the key and wiggle it and yell at it, but the door still doesn't open. Then you look again at the house number. "Oh," you realize, "our address is 405 Chestnut Circle." You go to the house next door. *There*, the door opens for you.

What does that open door mean to you? (Something you own; a place of your own.)

In a very positive letter to the church at Philadelphia, Jesus says in effect, "Look! I have set before you an open door." We'll take a closer look to see what that meant to the Philadelphians, and to us.

2
Open-and-Shut Case

(20 minutes)

Studying the
Philadelphia Story

If you passed out copies of Resource 18, "Destination: Philadelphia," last time, ask any who filled them out to help you with answers during this step.

Philadelphia was about 25 miles southeast of Sardis. It was located in a region known for vine-growing and a textile and leather industry. Its church was apparently very healthy.

Still, it did face the usual foes. Emperor worship was probably required, and various Greek and local gods would have been worshiped in the area. There was also a Jewish group in Philadelphia that caused problems for the church.

Ask someone to read Revelation 3:7.

How does Christ describe Himself? (Holy and true. The one who holds the key of David. What He opens stays open.)

Let's take a closer look at this description. In what way is Christ holy and true? (He is the holy God. He lived without sin. He is true to His word. He said, "I am the way and the truth and the life.")

Would the hearers of this letter feel good or bad about Jesus being "holy and true"? (It depends which side you're on. If He's against you, His holiness will point out your unholiness and He will be true to His word in judging you.)

What do you think this "key of David" is? (The power to rule God's people.)

Ask someone to turn to Isaiah 22:15, 17-22 and read it.

Explain: Shebna was sort of the secretary of state to the king. He had great power, but he was misusing it. So God says He will depose him and appoint a new secretary of state, Eliakim. This new person will have the "key to the house of David," the power of the royal office. But later God indicates that even Eliakim will fall from power. The message is clear: God controls the keys.

Now back to Philadelphia. Let's say you're one of the members of the active Jewish community there, and you hear this— Jesus holds the "key of David." How does it make you feel? (Mad! Jesus is claiming God's power. There is also the hint that God has transferred His favor to the Christians, as He transferred power from Shebna to Eliakim. The impact of this verse underscores the theme of Revelation: Jesus is in control.)

Ask someone to read verse 8.

There's our open door. But let's put it aside for a moment. What does Jesus "know" in this verse? (The Philadelphian Christians' deeds. They have little strength, but they've remained faithful.)

Now, what do you think this "open door" is all about? (Many like to think of it as a door for ministry and evangelism. Paul used the term with that meaning. It is also possible that the door symbolizes escape from the turmoil around them. The best option may be that it is the door to God's kingdom. God invites them in; they just need to keep moving toward it.)

Ask someone to read verse 9.

We have met these "so-called Jews" before, in Smyrna. There, too, they were called a "synagogue of Satan." This is not an anti-Semitic statement; it describes a particular group of Jews who caused problems for the Christians. What does Jesus say will ultimately happen to them? (They will fall at the feet of the Christians and acknowledge them.)

How would this happen? (Who knows? Maybe they would be converted. But more likely, this text is looking forward to the end time when "every knee should bow" [Philippians 2:10]. The Bible indicates that believers will "reign with" Christ.)

Have someone read verses 10 and 11.

How will Christ reward the faithful ones for their patient endurance? (By protecting them from the worldwide testing. Some feel this passage supports the idea that Jesus will return and remove believers before the Great Tribulation, but there are other ways to interpret it. The basic points remain: God protects His people in difficult times. A time of great testing will come. And, "I am coming soon.")

How do you think the Philadelphians would react to the promise "I am coming soon"? (With joy, relief, expectation.)

Now here's the tough question. That was 1900 years ago, and Christ still hasn't come back. Did He mean what He said? (Yes. There are two main ways to answer this. First is the definition of "soon." The Lord is on a very different time schedule. Peter tells us that a day, for the Lord, is like a thousand years. In that case, it's been almost two days since Revelation was written. His coming is the next big thing to happen. The second explanation is that the Lord "comes to us" spiritually in times of need. When we look for His help, His coming is always "soon." There is some comfort in this second explanation, but the hope of the first still stands. He has made clear that He is coming back to set things right. We still await that day.)

3
When the Role Is Played Up Yonder

(15 minutes)

Having Fun with the Idea of Expectation

You'll need three pairs of dramatically minded volunteers for an impromptu roleplay (or use the same pair more than once if the group is smaller). Give each pair one of the situations you've copied and cut from Resource 19, "Role-ing in Dough."

Give pairs about half a minute to read their situations. Then let each roleplay run from one to three minutes. Don't be afraid to cut the roleplays off if they're going nowhere. [Note: If your group can't improvise, just have pairs describe what might happen instead of trying to act it out.]

Enjoy the role-plays, and ask some questions afterward. **Each of these situations was abnormal in some way. Why?** (The expectation of a future change made the present circumstances obsolete.)

If the worker had *not* gotten another job, how would he have responded?

If the tourist did not have to get rid of her money, how would that transaction have taken place?

What changed when the debtor learned he had won the sweepstakes?

Now for the 64-Mervolian-dollar question: **How should our lives change when we realize that Jesus is coming soon?** (Like the first person, we have a new boss. We don't have to serve the forces of this world anymore. Like the second, we have a new currency. We know we "can't take it with us." Jesus said to store up our treasure in heaven. Like the third, our current problems seem trivial when we know great blessing awaits.)

4

Because He's Coming Back

(12 minutes)

Planning New Attitudes
and Actions in Light of
Christ's Return

Hand out Resource 14, "Because He's Coming Back." Introduce it in this way: **Let's look a bit closer at that question. What effect does it have on my thoughts and actions when I realize that Jesus is coming back? Fill out what you can on this sheet and then we'll talk about it.**

After five minutes or so, go over the sheet, asking about the attitude changes. Do not press for responses on the "specific action" questions. These may be private. Some possible answers follow.

Unbelievers (More urgency about sharing Christ with them.)

People responding negatively (Relax. Christ will ultimately vindicate His own.)

Temptation (Trust Christ's power to withstand it. You want to stay on His side.)

Day-to-day problems (Christ is in control. These problems are trivial. You'll have a wonderful eternity.)

Wrap it up: **Jesus says there's an open door in your future. He's going to invite you someday into His presence. Is that a door of escape from your current problems? Is it a door of opportunity? Is it a door that offers access to great wealth and comfort? Yes, yes, and yes. As you go through your life, see that open door ahead of you, and let that vision keep your spiritual fire going.**

Close in prayer, asking God to remind the group continually of Jesus' promise to return.

If you'd like to prepare people for next time, hand out copies of Resource 21, "Destination: Laodicea." Encourage group members to work through it, using any Bible study helps they may have as well as Scripture itself.

ROLE-ING IN DOUGH

Situation A: Person 1 has just learned that he's* been accepted at a new job, beginning next week. It pays better, with better conditions. He is planning to quit at the end of the week. Person 2 is the growly boss, who is hated by everyone in the office. The boss comes by to tell the employee to work harder.

Situation B: Person 1 is in the foreign country of Mervolia. She* is about to travel home, and has just learned that the Mervolian dollars are devaluing so fast that no one will change them for her own country's dollars. The money is essentially worthless outside of the country. She still has 100 Mervolian dollars to get rid of. Mervolian law prohibits the giving of gifts of more than 10 dollars. Person 2 is a street peddler in Mervolia, trying to sell Person 1 a tie. Normally it would sell for three Mervolian dollars, but the peddler is jacking the price up to six.

Situation C: Person 1 is a bill collector, demanding payment on overdue credit card bills from Person 2, who has fallen behind on his* payments and doesn't know where he'll find the money to pay. A minute into the conversation, the phone rings and Person 2 learns that he has just won the Publishers Clearing House sweepstakes. A check for one million dollars will be arriving within a week. He goes back to the conversation with Person 1, who finds this hard to believe.

* All roles may be played by either male or female.

BECAUSE HE'S COMING BACK

Jesus said, "I am coming soon!" How will that affect the way I think about the unbelievers I know?

What specific actions can I take this week to express that?

Jesus said, "I am coming soon!" How will that affect the way I react when people respond negatively to my Christianity, even mocking me?

Is there anything I can do specifically to express this attitude this week?

Jesus said, "I am coming soon!" How will that affect the way I behave when I am tempted to sin?

Is there anything I can do specifically to express this attitude this week?

Jesus said, "I am coming soon!" How will that affect the way I behave when I face day-to-day problems of money and relationships?

Is there anything I can do specifically to express this attitude this week?

DESTINATION: LAODICEA

RESOURCE 21

From a Commentary or Study Bible
Background on Laodicea:

From the text (Revelation 3:14-22)
How does Christ describe Himself?

What does He "know"?

Course of action:

LIFESTYLES OF THE RICH AND TASTELESS
Learning from the Church at Laodicea

What's the greatest obstacle to spiritual growth in our culture today?

I believe it's money.

We love it. We worship it. We change our lives to get more of it. We are in its power.

Of all the gods of our age—Sex, Mammon, Self, Fame—Mammon is the one that has wormed its way most deeply into our lives and loves. Most of us rarely challenge the notion that more is better. And we explain away Christ's many cautions about the dangers of worldly wealth.

In planning this session, I very nearly offered you this object lesson: "Ask a group member to give you a five-dollar bill. In front of the group, tear it in pieces. Talk about why that offends them." But I chickened out. Cash is too powerful a symbol. The point would be lost in the horror of it. (If you're brave, you may still try that. But be ready for strong responses. "We could have given that to the poor!" Yes, but *would* we have?)

This session does not demand that we sell our Volvos, wear holes in our Dockers, and live in a commune. Wealth is not evil, but it is dangerous. People tend to trust in their "stuff" more than in God.

That was apparently true of the Laodiceans. It may be true of us. We think we can have it all—affluence, convenience, spirituality—"We are rich!" Christ challenges us to look again at our relationship with Him and see how poor we are.

Where You're Headed:
To challenge group members to avoid the distractions of money and things and to serve Christ fully.

Scriptures You'll Apply:
Revelation 3:14-22

Things You'll Need:
- Bibles
- Play money
- Index cards with dollar amounts for *Deal of Fortune* (Step 1)
- Chalkboard and chalk, or newsprint or poster board and marker
- Pens or pencils
- Copies of "God and Money" (Resource 22)
- Copies of "Action Sheet" (Resource 23)
- "Vanna" volunteer (Step 1)

1
Deal of Fortune
(10 minutes)

Making Light of Money

Hello, everyone. And welcome to *Deal of Fortune!*
You'll be re-enacting the popular TV game show, *Wheel of Fortune*. You'll need a "Vanna" volunteer and three "contestants." You'll also need a stack of play money and a chalkboard (or poster board or newsprint) with blanks for the "hidden phrase" on it.

Instead of a wheel, "Vanna" will have a deck of index cards with dollar amounts on them from $100 to $1000. (Be sure to have a "Bankrupt" card in there, too.) When a player takes a turn, "Vanna" will deal a card to the player, and that will be the value of the consonants guessed.

Suggested first phrase: "Seek ye first God's kingdom." If the game is going well, try a second or third. Suggestions: "Treasure in heaven"; "You cannot serve God and Money."

As the players guess consonants (and buy vowels), fill them in on the board until a player is ready to guess the whole phrase. Hand the proper amount of play money to each contestant after each successful guess.

At the end of the game, offer the winner a chance to buy prizes. These prizes are, of course, more or less worthless.

Suggested prize list:

$200—A church bulletin (a feast of information, it also makes a dandy airplane!)

$300—A stick of gum (pure chewing satisfaction!)

$500—A paper clip (not only can you bend it into artistic designs, it also cleans the dirt from under your fingernails!)

$1000—A trip to the rest room (with the finest accommodations!)

$1500—A lifetime supply of "Resource sheets" from the David C. Cook Publishing Company (with permission to copy them over and over!)

Add other prizes appropriate to your group. When the merriment is dying down, talk about it:

What happened here? We played a silly game. This person won the game and got a lot of money. This money was then used to buy things that were essentially worthless.

In the context of the game, this person is rich. We lavished attention on him (or her). He (or she) was the big winner. But once this person steps out of the room, it doesn't matter. Different rules apply.

What happens if he (or she) goes to the corner store and says, "Give me a newspaper; here's $500," and hands the clerk this play money? It won't work.

The same thing is true of our earthly lives. In a way, we're playing a game here. Some people get a lot of money. For the moment, they're the winners. They can buy a lot of things that are, in the long run, worthless. It may not be a paper clip; it may be a yacht. But step out of this world, and that yacht doesn't mean a thing. All that wealth is just play money, when you look at it from God's eternal perspective.

For our winner to think, "I'm rich!" because he (or she) has a handful of play money would be foolish. It's just as foolish for a

millionaire to think a portfolio of blue-chip investments makes him or her rich in God's eyes. Today we're going to meet a church that made that mistake.

2 The Eyes Have It
(5 minutes)

Getting Some Background on Laodicea

If you passed out copies of Resource 21, "Destination: Laodicea," last time, ask any who filled them out to help you with answers during the next two steps.

The seventh church of Revelation was at Laodicea. This city was forty-five miles southeast of Philadelphia. It lay along an important trade route stretching from Ephesus through the inland area of what is now Turkey. It was located in a valley along with two "sister cities," Colosse and Hierapolis.

There were three major industries in Laodicea. (If possible, write these on the board as you say them.)

First, banking. It was an extremely wealthy city. After an earthquake in A.D. 17 devastated the area, the Roman Empire pitched in financially to help many of the cities. But Laodicea refused this aid and chose to rebuild itself.

Second, eye care. There was an ointment produced in Laodicea that was famous for curing eye ailments.

Third, textiles. The city produced a special black wool that was popular throughout the empire.

One other thing you should know about this city: For all their wealth, they had a frustrating water problem. (Write this on the board, too.) They had no water source nearby. They had to pipe in their water from a spring six miles south. We're not sure whether this was a cold spring or a hot spring. But it didn't matter, because as it traveled the six-mile aqueduct, it cooled (or heated) to a lukewarm temperature.

3 Hot and Cold
(20 minutes)

Figuring Out What Went Wrong in Laodicea

Ask someone to read Revelation 3:14.

What does Christ call Himself? (The Amen, the faithful and true witness, the ruler of God's creation.)

The Amen—what's that about? (Amen is a Hebrew word for "Yes," "That's right," or "So be it." We're talking affirmation. It's something you say to God to indicate that you're willing to go along with what He says.)

Why does Christ call Himself the "Amen, the faithful and true witness"? (He is trustworthy. What He promises, He will do. The blessings and judgments that God has promised will come true in Christ.)

Why does He call Himself the "ruler of all creation"? (The word for ruler is literally "first." He's in charge. Everything and everyone answers to Him.)

Ask someone to read verses 15 and 16.

What does Christ "know"? (Their deeds.)

Why do you think He uses this image of "lukewarm"? (Perhaps because they had a lukewarm water supply.)

What does He mean by that? What are "cold" and "hot" deeds? What kind of deeds does He want? (It's best not to define "cold" and "hot" as "bad" and "good." Both cold and hot water were useful; lukewarm water was not. Because the Laodiceans were so wishy-washy, they were useless to the Lord, and distasteful.)

Ask someone to read verse 17.

What was the church's attitude? (Confident, secure, complacent.)

What was their real situation? (Needy, desperate.)

How would the Laodiceans react to the way Christ describes them—wretched, pitiful, poor, blind, and naked? (They would be offended and embarrassed. They were wealthy. How could He call them "wretched, pitiful" or "poor"? They had the finest eye medicines. How could He call them blind? They produced beautiful clothing. How could they be naked? All their material wealth was insignificant in light of their spiritual needs.)

Why do you think they did not realize how needy they were? (Their material wealth could blind them to their spiritual needs.)

Have someone read verse 18.

What does He want them to do? (Come to Him for help.)

What is the significance of the three things He offers them? (They are "new, improved" brands of things that the Laodiceans already had. The gold is refined by fire—perhaps the fire of persecution that would result from being true to Christ. The clothing is the robes of Christ's righteousness. The eye salve is not their famous medicine, but Christ's healing touch.)

How would the Laodiceans get this gold, this clothing, this eye salve? (By coming to Christ in repentance. By committing themselves to Him.)

Have someone read verses 19 and 20.

Why do you think God disciplines those He loves? (He wants them to have fellowship with Him, to learn to live life fully.)

How does He rebuke and discipline us? (Often He rebukes us through His messengers, our ministers and teachers. Obviously, this letter to Laodicea is a rebuke. He disciplines us often by allowing us to reap the fruit of our own sinful deeds. Sin leads to ruin. Sometimes we have to experience that to learn it.)

What do the Laodiceans need to do? (Be earnest and repent. The word for "earnest" is the word for "zealous." The Lord is saying, in effect, "Get excited about Me! No more of this wishy-washy stuff!")

What kind of relationship does Christ want to have with them? (He wants to be welcome in their lives, to be a friend to them, like someone they'd invite to dinner.)

Last time we talked about open doors. Christ sets before us an open door, the door to His kingdom. But now the tables are turned. He is knocking on a closed door. He wants us to open our door and let Him into our lives.

You may be familiar with this verse as an evangelistic appeal: "Let Christ into your heart. Accept Him as your Savior." But He's talking to a church. These people already profess to be

Christians. He's saying, "Let Me into your life! I want to be part of what you do each day. I want to be important to you."
Is He saying that to you right now?

4
Money Talks
(15 minutes)

Seeing How Wealth
Can Get in the Way

Hand out copies of Resource 22, "God and Money."

Divide into three groups. Assign a different situation to each group. Give groups five minutes or so to read the situations and discuss their responses. Then bring the whole group back together and share results.

There may be several valid responses. Here are some suggested ones:

(*Richard Prince*—It's amazing how often Scripture violates common sense. It would make sense to find a more reasonable church or to make a partial sacrifice. But if the Lord is telling Rich Prince to give it all away, he'd better obey. Or is that just for biblical characters?

Martha Tally—She worries too much. Frank should probably do more than spout off Bible verses, but he's right. Worrying doesn't help. God will take care of them. They may need to simplify their lifestyle. That may not be fun, but worrying isn't fun either.

Stephanie Silver—She could learn an important lesson here. Her desire to obey God should not be squelched. If it's truly her money, she should be able to do what she wants with it. To learn sacrificial giving, she would need to do without ice cream. Mom should loosen up and rejoice in her daughter's youthful zeal.)

5
Accounting for Ourselves
(10 minutes)

Finding Ways That Wealth
Keeps Us from God

Hand out Resource 23, "Action Sheet."

Give people a few minutes to fill it out individually. If you sense they are willing, and if there's time, talk about some of the questions. (You might pick your favorite one and pursue it.)

Rather than trying to tell group members how to use their money, or trying to reach consensus, help them listen for God's direction.

There are no easy answers to most of the questions on this sheet. God's answers may be different for two people facing the same situation. The point is to get people to face their own attitudes and wrestle with changes they might need to make.

6
Who's That Knocking? (optional)

(10 minutes)

Wrapping Up the Course

If time allows, you might wrap up the whole course as follows.

Jesus stands at the door and knocks. He calls, "Let Me in. I want to dine with you."

Based on what we learned of the seven churches, how might each of them reply? Various responses are possible; share the following as needed.

The church in Ephesus ("Who's that knocking? I don't seem to remember that voice.")

The church in Smyrna ("It might be a Roman soldier coming to get me, but I'm not afraid.")

The church in Pergamum ("Sorry, we're having a meeting of the Nicolaitan Society in here.")

The church in Thyatira ("Go away. Jezebel and I are . . . uh . . . indisposed.")

The church in Sardis ("Didn't we have dinner once, a long time ago? I'm not hungry anymore.")

The church in Philadelphia ("Come right in, Lord. I've been waiting for You.")

The church in Laodicea ("Sorry, I'm going out to dinner at a fancy restaurant. Maybe some other time.")

What does your church say?

What do you as an individual say?

As we've seen in this course, many things can act as "wet blankets" on our spiritual fire. Many things can distract us from having fellowship with Jesus.

But Christ is the "ruler of all creation." He wants to have first place in our lives—and deserves it.

Close in prayer, asking God to speak to each group member, and that Christ would come in and dine with every receptive heart.

GOD AND MONEY

Situation A: Richard Prince

I've been very fortunate. Oh, I've worked hard, but I've had lots of breaks along the way. I got my MBA and started a business; it's gone extremely well.

Excellence—that's my goal. In my work, in my personal life. I drive a fine car, own two fine homes, eat fine food. Things are just fine for me right now.

A friend invited me to come to his church, and I did. I liked what I saw. There was a spiritual energy there that I wanted. The pastor was a bit odd, but he made sense. Before long I decided to become a Christian.

So I told this pastor, "I'd like to get really committed to this church. What do I have to do?"

To my surprise, he said, "That's good. But you need to sell all you have and donate it to the poor."

It was the craziest thing I'd ever heard. I mean, he should have been happy to welcome me. But as I thought about it, it was like there was this weight on top of me. It was like God Himself was saying, "Do it. Do it. Give it all up."

Now I don't know what to do.

    What should he do?
____ Sell his stuff.
____ Find a different church.
____ Sell some of his stuff and make a big donation.
____ Other (explain)

    What would you say to him?

Situation B: Martha Tally

It's a struggle to make ends meet in our home. With three growing kids, two incomes is hardly enough. We go broke just buying sneakers for these kids.

My husband, Frank, doesn't understand. I'm the math whiz in our home, so I write the checks. And I worry. I have to.

The simple fact is that we're one catastrophe away from bankruptcy. If Brendan needs braces or if the refrigerator dies or if the roof springs a leak, we're done for.

It keeps me up nights, but doesn't seem to bother Frank. He keeps quoting me Bible verses. "Don't worry about tomorrow," he says. "Tomorrow has enough worries of its own." And then he rolls over and goes back to sleep. Frank just doesn't understand, or he doesn't care.

    Who has the better perspective?
____ He does. She worries too much.
____ She does. He's too naive.
____ They need to meet in the middle.

    What would you say to them?

(CONTINUED)

GOD AND MONEY (CONT.)

Situation C: Stephanie Silver, age 8

Mom can be really weird sometimes. Last Saturday, she gave me two dollars and said we could go out for ice cream Sunday afternoon and I could buy anything I wanted with those two bucks. (I think she's trying to teach me about money.)

So, anyway, we went to church on Sunday and I sat with Mom, like I always do. When the offering plate went around, Mom put a couple of dollars in it.

I thought about giving my two dollars. But then I thought about the ice cream—mint chocolate chip—and decided not to put the money in the plate.

But then the pastor preached about how it was important to give our whole lives to God. Even stuff that was really important to us. Like ice cream.

So after church I went up to the pastor and gave him my two dollars and said I wanted God to have it.

Later, when I told Mom what I did, she got mad. She said the money was a gift, and she wanted me to keep it. So we never did go out for ice cream.

What should Mom have done?
_____ What she did was fine.
_____ Get the money back from the pastor.
_____ Go out for ice cream anyway.
_____ Talk with Stephanie to make sure she knew what she was doing.
_____ Go out for ice cream, but not let Stephanie have any.
_____ Praise the girl for doing this.
_____ Other (explain)

What would you say to Stephanie or to her Mom?

ACTION SHEET

Answer these questions as honestly as you can. They are designed to challenge you, perhaps to change you.

1. Which do you spend more time doing? Worrying about money or reading the Bible?

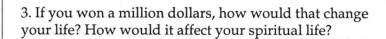

2. If someone offered you an amount equal to your yearly income to stay away from church for a year, would you do it? Would you consider it?

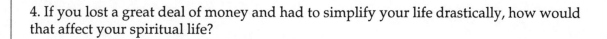

3. If you won a million dollars, how would that change your life? How would it affect your spiritual life?

4. If you lost a great deal of money and had to simplify your life drastically, how would that affect your spiritual life?

5. You're in a northern city in the dead of winter. You have a brand new, fairly expensive overcoat. As you near your hotel, a beggar asks you for your coat. He is freezing. Do you give it? Why or why not?

6. If you got paid to read the Bible and pray, would you do more of it?

7. Two situations: (a) Your children grow up to be fairly wealthy, but their Christianity is stagnant; (b) your children grow up to be poor, but spiritually dynamic. Which would you prefer?

8. If your income were cut by 25%, how would you cut your expenses? Would you be able to do that if you had to? Would you ever consider cutting your expenses by 25% and giving the savings to feed the hungry?

The intent of this quiz is not to make you feel guilty, nor to make you give more to the church. It is merely to help you gauge your relationship with God in comparison with your relationship with money. God will let you know how He wants you to use whatever wealth you have. Are you ready to listen to Him?